Logic and Faith

Westminster Studies in Christian Communication
Kendig Brubaker Cully, General Editor

Logic
and Faith

A Study of the Relations Between Science and Religion

WALTER E. STUERMANN

THE WESTMINSTER PRESS

Philadelphia

To
LUCILLE
with love

Contents

A Note on Westminster Studies
in Christian Communication

These Studies are predicated on the ground that the Christian faith needs to be made relevant to persons in the modern world in terms of the dynamic nature of the faith itself and the channels that are capable of conveying such a faith. In itself any technique of communication conceivably could serve as well for secular as for religious ends. In this series a wide variety of means and methods of communication will be analyzed in the light of their availability to, and suitability for, the particular tasks that the Christian church faces in bringing the realities of faith to bear upon the life of actual persons in the contemporary situation.

Oftentimes in the past, techniques have been viewed almost as ends in themselves. Or, they have been taken over uncritically from the secular culture without being subjected to adequate scrutiny as to whether they are appropriate for the church's use. On the other hand, sometimes the church has been blind to the life situations of the present to such an extent as to ignore the real ways in which people's lives are influenced by all that impinges on them. In the latter case, the church has failed to bring the life-giving power of the gospel to bear on contemporary culture because of a lack of understanding of, or appreciation for, the means of communication that have been proved capable of changing lives and societies.

Involving as it does both the " What " and the " How," the whole question of the communication of the gospel in the modern world is pivotal in the present juncture of history. The present Studies will be aimed at bringing the " What " and the " How " together fruitfully. These books are designed to make a contribution to the ongoing conversations across boundaries. Theology, Biblical studies, sociology, cultural anthropology, psychology, education, art, letters, science, and the other disciplines all have something to say to one another. In our present concern, "communication" refers to the way in which the Christian faith can come into conjunction with what is happening in the total world of life and ideas in the middle decades of the twentieth century. In each of these Studies attention will focus on some important aspect of the basic question: How can the church most effectively preach, teach, and otherwise manifest the gospel in the growing edges of man's present-day culture? No aspect of man's actual situation is alien to such a question. No medium of communication should fail to come under scrutiny if, as Christians, we are eager to have the Word of God confront a confused generation powerfully and compellingly.

Each volume in Westminster Studies in Christian Communication will be an authentic voice of one perceptive interpreter. No effort has been made to suggest to any writer what "line" he ought to follow. Each work will be adjudged by the readers on its own merits. The writers themselves conceivably might disagree heartily with regard to certain presuppositions or conclusions held by their colleagues. All this will be to the good if the result of these Studies should be the stimulating of many conversations. Yet all the writers have in mind a focus that is realistic, an emphasis that is practical, and a discussion that is timely. The only request made of the authors is that they speak out of their knowledge to the very heart and mind of our times. Depth without dullness, breadth without diffuseness, challenge without sentimentality — these, at least, it is hoped, will be characteristics of all the Studies. We are grateful to those who have consented to share in this venture into communication, and we commend their work as in itself an integral part of the church's task of communication.

KENDIG BRUBAKER CULLY
General Editor

Evanston, Illinois

Preface

The rise of modern scientific method has transfigured our civilization. A man can scarcely move a foot these days without stubbing his toes against some mechanism produced by the application of scientific method. The achievements of modern science and technology are among the most notable marks of contemporary Western culture. Today men thrash about in the world among skyscrapers and submarines, electric toasters and electronic calculators, ballistic missiles and the mechanical marvels of automation. Overawed by the Promethean powers of science, many are inclined to make short work of disposing of their religious heritage. Are their judgments that one cannot be sincerely religious and also scientific in action and outlook justified? A mixed multitude think so. This is the question that the present book examines. It attempts to do so without presupposing a definitive answer and without moving finally and confidently to one.

The writer advances an analysis of some of the relations between science and religion. He does not attempt to "reconcile" them systematically, assuming that their interests and aims have been completely alien to each other. Nor does he believe that they are completely compatible, or that they are polar opposites. While contending that each has its own distinctive method for seeking knowledge and guiding conduct, the author argues that the two disciplines can at certain points supplement each other.

11

The accent throughout the analysis is on the *logic* of scientific inquiry and the *logical structure and significance* of religious thinking and acting. There is no attempt to produce a system of thought within which all tensions would be resolved and all problems solved. By comparing and contrasting the underlying logics of inquiry in the two disciplines, the writer attempts to shed some light on a few problems that arise in the relations between these two important aspects of human life. In this way he seeks to promote communication between men of faith and men of science. The conviction that both scientific and religious inquiries are open-ended processes expresses itself throughout the presentation. Science and religion are essentially methods of thinking and acting, not primarily bodies of knowledge. There are no final conclusions to be concluded: hence, the accent here on the logics of science and religion. In the measure, however, that these two methods or logics are discovered to be compatible with each other, clear and meaningful communication can be fostered between the Christian faith and modern science.

Since the author has tried to write simply about science and religion, the discussion does not bristle with differential equations or triple-jointed words. He trusts that the endeavor for simplicity has not become a conspiracy resulting in many inaccuracies. Judgment on that issue, of course, must be left to the reader.

McCormick Quarterly, McCormick Theological Seminary, Chicago, has kindly granted permission for the use of a revised form of " The Human Prospect when God Is Dead " (Volume XIV, Number 2) in Chapter XI. A section of Chapter VII which deals with certain cardinal virtues was used in a different context in *Philosophy and the American Heritage*, by the author and Johnson D. Hill. Philosophical Library, Inc., New York, has been gracious enough to permit this material to be recast into a different mold for use here. Apart from these passages and a few other citations, the reader is redeemed from severe oppression under footnotes. The writer has tried to make

13

the presentation sound and scholarly, but he has not wanted to be nasty about it.

The author expresses his gratitude to Margaret Kelley, Louise Larrabee, and Carolyn Shirley for their help in the reading of proof and the preparation of the index. He is especially appreciative of the continuing philosophical conversation in which he is engaged with his colleague, Dr. Paul L. Brown of the University of Tulsa, a number of whose ideas have unquestionably made themselves felt in this presentation.

W.E.S.

University of Tulsa
Tulsa, Oklahoma

Chapter I

Introduction

The frightening din of the common alarm clock, awakening us from blessed unconsciousness with a daily shock to our nervous systems, is a part and sign of the noisy, lethal haste of our civilization. That alarm clock is one of the simpler mechanical blessings that modern science has bestowed upon us. It makes its own little contribution to the elimination of the serene life we all rather wistfully contemplate for ourselves. Nevertheless, modern science has brought to us many conveniences and freedom from countless handicaps and diseases. It therefore justly requests our defense of its integrity and its freedom of inquiry. Many men are insufficiently grateful for the pleasures, comforts, and security that science has produced for us. Yet that monstrous clock plagues us. It makes us prompt for appointments, but often shatters our nerves. It is an ambivalent gadget, as are most of the machines and tools that distinguish our civilization. The automatic pistol can be used to kill a poisonous snake, but also to slay a man. The airplane can facilitate communication and effect rescues, but it can also be used to strafe villages. Some disinfectants, judiciously used, can protect health; on the other hand, the same can be used to commit suicide. Actually, the gadget itself is not ambivalent. The men who use the gadgets are double-valued. They are able to create or to destroy with them. They can enhance peace and health or destroy these blessings with the intricate machines science has put into their hands. In any case, it is clear to everyone that our civilization is one of many machines, of great haste, and of much anxiety and noise.

Much of our frenetic pace and its consequent distresses are due to the fact that men have not quite come to terms with the scientific achievements of our day. Many openmouthed defenders and avid admirers of science have little understanding of scientific method. The combination of admiration and ignorance is a witches' brew. Having partaken of it, man goes on a spree and turns his machines to destructive uses. His life is an irresponsible carousal among machines of which he has little real understanding. Even if he did understand them, he would still in great measure be morally incompetent to turn their powers to creative and humane uses.

It has also been softly whispered here and there that the rise of science in the last two centuries has brought with it a secular spirit and a suspicion of the validity of many of our traditional religious aspirations, ideas, and practices. By and large, this is true. It *is* rather difficult to maintain a reverent attitude in the midst of a raucous culture. It is hard to see the relevance for this day of religious ideas and ideals that were brought forth thousands of years ago. Only the most hearty varieties of religious faith can survive at a time when men are preoccupied with nuclear fission and fusion and mechanical brains. Who can be compassionate when he is thrust disjointedly into a noisy, crowded suburban train? Who can maintain interest in rather illogical, sentimental religious discourses when he realizes that it has been the exercise of unprejudiced reason that has produced a civilization replete with refrigerators, television, and jet propulsion? It is almost inevitable that a man's interest be captured by the machines that make a continuous, concrete impact upon his life, from alarm clock in the morning, through automat luncheon, to electrically warmed blanket at night. The kingdom of the machine is among us.

No wonder there has been a rash of literature in recent years trying rather anxiously to reconcile science and religion. Many fear that the moral and religious values that gave cohesion to our common life are in jeopardy. The matter has even come to the attention of many of the popular journals.

Reconciling religion and science is, however, no recently invented game, though many so believe. Christian thinkers in every century have been called upon to rethink and restate their positions as a result of the impact of new knowledge and new ideas. This is precisely what such men as Origen, Aquinas, Descartes, Leibnitz, and Berkeley did in their days and in their ways. It is a game played in every age — a necessary game and an edifying one. It was invented long before the furors stirred up by the appearances of the scientific hypotheses of evolution and relativity. It is appropriate and right that Christian men should want to speak of the values of their faith in terms that make sense to contemporary science. As a matter of fact, it is necessary, if religious faith is not to be made superfluous by being outrun by human knowledge.

Some recent contestants in the game either have no knowledge of the rules of the contest or do not have the spirit of sportsmanship which keeps it healthy and honest. Many unsober and insane words have been written reconciling Genesis and science (as if they needed to be reconciled). Three criticisms may be made of many recent discussions of the relations between science and religion. First, some of them have been produced in an uncritical, partisan spirit, with the result that justice is not done to one of the disciplines. One of the contesting teams in the game has been unfairly subsidized. Secondly, there is often a lack of real understanding on the part of the author either of scientific method or of the nature and values of religious experience and literature. Thirdly, sometimes the discussions are written in a jargon that requires an Oppenheimer or a Thomas Aquinas to understand them. Immanuel Velikovsky's *Worlds in Collision* (1950) is a striking example of what can be done to confuse the issue if one has not disciplined his statements by available facts or fails to handle historical and legendary materials in a critical way. Men who ask questions about the relations between science and religion are not interested in discovering the fertility of the writer's imagination but in getting a reliable and useful point of view on these two aspects of life and culture. There is no occasion here for "speaking in tongues," whether with or without the Spirit. A right understanding of both science and religion is essential for man's physical and spiritual health. One ought to be able to discuss such a critical matter in sober and simple words.

To say these ill-natured things about many of the attempts to reconcile science and religion is to be exceptionally reserved in our judgment. A more damning and disastrous word can be uttered. This distraught world is sick unto death. Some of the symptoms of its sickness are war, moral insensitivity, suspicion, prejudice, and cruelty. Physically and spiritually, its life is in jeopardy. In the words of Hebrews, it " shrinks back in fear to destruction." Nothing less than a thorough moral and spiritual rejuvenation is required in the withering patient. A religion that is to act as therapy for this patient must be a potent reviver of life and health, not a drug to deaden the nerves against pain. No ordinary attempt to reconcile science and religion, assuming that they are at heart alien to each other, will provide the requisite resurrection of spirit. A reconciliation of science and religion that proceeds along traditional lines will give the patient only momentary relief from pain. But the pain will return, and the illness, which is its source, will run its deadly course. The cure of the illness requires surgery and long postsurgical therapy. Those who continue the conventional reconciliation either are ignorant of the patient's problem or are deceiving him as to what his difficulty is.

Consequently, the interpretation of science and religion that follows will not be focused mainly upon the antique theme: Genesis versus science. In passing, let it be said about this issue and about the whole matter of the relation of science to the testimonies of the Biblical literature that the conventional attack upon the problem is a vain one. Bulky books used to be written in an attempt to prove that science authenticated the stories of origins recorded in Gen., chs. 1 to 11. The rivers ran into the sea, but the sea was not filled. The authors of these abortive treatises wasted much time and energy. They wasted it, because they misconstrued the problem at the outset. They committed the error of thinking that the passages of the Biblical literature were objective historical and scientific documents that could be verified by summoning appropriate factual evidence. If the writings are scientific documents, then they can be warranted in this way. But they are not history or science. Put it this way. A man who tries to reconcile Genesis and science assumes either that Genesis is science or that science is religion. On either score he is wrong. Science is a discipline of inquiry that has its own distinctive subject matters and methods, different from those of religion. A religious document is the literary precipitate of inspiration. It expresses the outpouring of affections toward God. Consequently, it is a poetic and devotional literature. Other rules of analysis and evaluation must be used for it than those employed on the problems encountered in building bridges.

There cannot be a real problem here, since we have two different disciplines dealing with two different kinds of subject matters. One has a real problem on his hands only when there are conflicting opinions and judgments about the same thing. Genesis and science cannot be reconciled, because there are no conflicting theories to be reconciled. No sober or sane man tries to substantiate scientifically Dante's *Divine Comedy* or Milton's *Paradise Lost;* nor does he think that all the meaning of such inspired works can be discovered by a literal, scientific interpretation of the words, phrases, and sentences. The meaning of poetry is seized chiefly through an intuitive apprehension of meaning, by a sensitivity to the allusions of metaphor, by the music of the rhythm, by an emotional rapport with the literary symphony. It is precisely a scientific dissection of poetic literature that is most likely to miss its meaning. The inspired writer did not intend to furnish a cadaver for microscopic analysis and for practice with the scalpel. No doubt

others will continue similar attempts to reconcile poetic Biblical texts with the logical discourses of science. Men remain enchanted by false problems long after those have been unmasked. But let us shake the dust of our feet against them
and go on.

It is most important for the survival of a vital, relevant religion that it be able to address itself clearly to a hectic civilization and to people mesmerized by science. If it cannot speak
clearly and sanely to such a time and such a people, it really
has nothing whatever to say. It will be firing blank cartridges
— a lot of noise but no lead. In every age, Christian thinkers
must take up the task of Friedrich Schleiermacher (1768–
1834), lately in considerable eclipse, when he issued his
Speeches on Religion to Its Cultured Despisers. Perhaps the
task today is, however, to address the uncultured despisers, ob-
serving the rather thorough ignorance of Biblical literature on
the part of the man on the street corner and the man in the
laboratory. In the pulpit or in the home, on the street corner
or in the classroom, one cannot assume anything in the way of
a sound knowledge of the Jewish-Christian literature and religion. On the other hand, one cannot assume that much real
information about scientific method lies behind modern man's
reverent contemplation of science. Unfortunately, many who
have developed an adolescent fondness for science have some-
how been deceived into developing a suspicion or outright
hatred toward their Christian heritage. This is largely due to
an ignorance of the real meaning of both science and religion.
The old problem of science and religion is, therefore, not
merely a technical, abstract one; it is the problem of making
men's lives whole and healthy and of making our civilization
sane and integral. If the man of faith has nothing sensible to
say about how science and religion are related, each co-operat-
ing with the other for a healthy, vital, and virtuous life, then
he ought to remain silent.

We have commented that science and religion are two different kinds of disciplines and that they deal with different

sorts of subject matters. The development of these points is, of course, to come later. Granting the contention now, is there any hope, then, of relating them? Are there some immediate indications that such a hope is justified? Yes. After all, both enterprises are probings by the same human being, employing the same mental and physical resources. Both disciplines are attempts to satisfy human inquisitiveness. Moreover, both of them are, at their lowest levels, rooted in first-person experience. Secondly, both types of inquiry have as their goal some comprehension or seizure of truth, although they may seek it in different ways. And thirdly, when each pursues its goal as it ought to be pursued, it is characterized by an admirable modesty and humility. It is this humble, inquisitive attitude, common to the two, which holds out great promise that the partisans of faith and of science can come to terms that will preserve integrity and health on both sides.

The basic humility of scientific inquirers is not often enough recognized and appreciated, especially in religious quarters. It is precisely this humility which restrains the scientist from launching out into speculative and metaphysical lines of thought that many religious persons wish him to follow. Modesty in thought and statement is, however, what keeps the scientist's discipline honest, reliable, and productive. He must be humble enough to submit himself to the available evidence and to let it alone guide his thought. He must be temperate in thought and action, so that he does not produce superstition rather than knowledge and destroy rather than create. He must be cautious in thought and assertion, lest he deceive himself and others and thus contribute to human ignorance and misery. The humility or modesty that underlies the scientist's reticence to speak and act quickly must be admired and preserved if the values he protects and sustains by his work are to be retained. The man of science is, in a real sense, reverent in the presence of truth. There are, of course, arrogant scientists, and there are scientists who make downright fools of themselves when they succumb to the temptation to make firm judgments outside their fields of specialization. But, to the extent that they are thus arrogant and undiscerning, they bear the name of science without possessing its spirit. A dogmatic and insensitive " scientist " is as much a hypocrite and a false prophet as is a dogmatic and cruel " Christian."

As we have suggested, we shall not presume to reconcile science and religion systematically. Our task will be to arrive at a simple understanding of scientific and religious inquiries and to use that understanding to deal with some problems that arise in their relationship to each other. We offer here no system through which the word-weary reader must plow. Systems are too boring and uncompromising anyway, particularly theological and philosophical ones. Problems are " solved " too neatly and quickly in systems. As Nietzsche once observed, the system builder is a deceiver. The only systems of thought that delight the mind and heart and do so with simplicity and elegance are mathematical ones. Systems of thought are possible in mathematics and logic because no question of truth is involved. One deals there with abstract ideas and their relations, not with irrevocable facts and recalcitrant persons. But more of this later. We abandon the systems to the presumptuous heirs of Thomas Aquinas and Georg Wilhelm Hegel.

While we consider it foolhardy to try to reconcile religion and science systematically, nevertheless we can give assurance that man is not in the dilemma of Buridan's ass. This miserable creature found itself poised equidistant from two enticing stacks of hay, one on each side. It perished from hunger, not being able to make the decision as to which it should eat from first. If it had been transfixed between two boa constrictors, instead of two bales of hay, its death — or at least a nervous breakdown — would have been understandable. Its dilemma is not well-founded psychologically. Neither is the science-religion dilemma a sound one. Man need not perish when he finds science on his right and religion on his left. Without anxiety and without shame, he can partake of both and thrive on the mixed diet.

As we proceed, some may think that we make things too difficult for religion. In part, this is deliberate. Men ought to be most critical of what they prize most highly, lest it be corrupted while they are complacently looking the other way. Not to criticize one's faith is to admit that it is not really very important. We cannot afford to be intellectually at ease in matters of faith. We must have the courage to examine our convictions.

Chapter II

In the Beginning of Science
Is the Fact

"Let's have the facts!" This is one of the insistent demands of our sophisticated generation. Everyone has and wants facts, uses and reveres facts. It is a mark of learning to cite facts to support one's opinions and to defend one's arguments. It is a fact that water was transformed into wine at Cana. The fact is that Jefferson was a deist. It is a fact that President Truman wrote a nasty letter to the Marine Corps. As a matter of fact, mercury is 13.6 times as heavy as water. Many facts support the doctrine of the assumption of Mary into heaven. It is a fact, according to the editor of one of our metropolitan newspapers, that Einstein was a subversive person. It is a fact that the tree will fall tomorrow when its trunk is severed. It is a fact that Spinoza wrote a book called *Ethics,* that Abraham existed, and that there are green dragons living on Mt. Ararat. According to the opinions of men, some of the weirdest superstitions and some of the most modest assertions have been supported by facts. The word "fact" has come to cover a multitude of things, so that nowadays we can have as little confidence in the "facts" cited by men as in the opinions they are supposed to support.

Modern science begins its sober inquiries into the nature of the world and life by dealing with facts. The term is, however, in such sad semantic circumstances these days that it is quite necessary to define precisely what a scientist means by it. Moreover, an adequate and exact definition of a scientific fact reveals much about the nature and competence of scientific method.

The sciences can be divided roughly into *formal* sciences and *factual* sciences. Mathematics and logic are formal sciences. They are concerned with rules of thought and calculation which are everywhere applicable. They do not deal with facts but with ideas, such as those of equality, straight line, number, inclusion, and continuity. Their object is to study how such ideas can be related to one another in consistent or formally correct argument. The plane geometry (Euclidean geometry) to which many students are exposed in high school is a simple but good example of a mathematical system. Such a system is purely theoretical. It does not have to refer to anything, that is, to any factual stuff. The formulation of other, non-Euclidean geometries (for example, those of Lobachevski and Riemann), which are exact and consistent, bears out this contention. Euclidean geometry does, however, have applications to things, for we can use it to calculate areas, volumes, and lengths of things in the world. This is not essential to it as a geometric system. The applicability of any mathematical system is something independent of the formal structure of the system and of the rules of thought employed in it. There are clear, consistent, and elegant mathematical systems that have no applications at all. Bertrand Russell once said that the mathematician does not know what he is talking about and does not care. The mathematician and logician are not primarily concerned with truth, that is, with whether the ideas they use correspond to things or whether the assertions they make are corroborated by relations among facts. They are chiefly interested in whether or not ideas and propositions are correctly related to one another in argument. We will later discuss in more detail this crucial distinction between truth and validity.

The other group of sciences is the collection of factual sciences. They deal with facts rather than exclusively with ideas. They handle the data supplied to consciousness by our nervous systems. To be more specific, these sciences operate with such sensory data as colors, tastes, sounds, and senses of weight, motion, and extension. Physics and chemistry are two of the most highly developed of the factual sciences. Others are biology, archaeology, history, and psychology. Each of these disciplines may have numerous subdivisions, reflecting the intensive specialization in modern science. There are, of course, significant differences among the factual sciences in the matter of the exactness with which they can talk about their data and in the matter of the number and precision of the tools with which they do their work. All of them are, however, concerned with truth. They want to know what facts can be found to support propositions such as " Copper wire increases in length with a rise in temperature " or " The city of Bethel was destroyed by nomads in the thirteenth century B.C."

Facts are needed to determine the truth of assertions, or at least to determine their usefulness. Just what is a fact? Before we try to answer this question, we should note that, as one passes from one science to another, there are differences in the degrees of exactness and reliability of the facts considered. A fact in psychology is usually somewhat more inexact or elusive than one in physics. It is in physics and chemistry that the nature of a scientific fact is best displayed. Nevertheless, it is fair to say that other sciences, such as history, biology, and psychology, which have not had so long a history behind them and have not developed so many refined tools for measurement, attempt to achieve the degree of refinement and exactness in their subject matters that is to be found in those of physics and chemistry. Whatever differences there may be among a piece of pottery, an approach-avoidance behavior pattern, and a mass of mercury, there are, nevertheless, certain features that they have in common that make them facts in a scientific sense of the word.

Here we shall try to describe the *positive* criteria for a scientific fact. In the following chapter, we shall state what a fact is not; that is, we shall make some critical remarks about the nature of a fact in order to show its limitations and to indicate why science is prevented from making metaphysical and theological judgments. The positive criteria for a fact are three in number, and they are very simple.

1. A scientific fact is based upon a sensory experience, such as visual sensations of extension, motion, or color; tactual sensations of extension, motion, or weight; and auditory sensations of shrillness or dullness. However refined the fact may become as a result of analysis and measurement, it is founded upon such a *qualitative* experience. Apples appear to be red, green, or yellow; the room feels warm or cold; the ball seems light or heavy; the whistle is heard as shrill; the pinprick feels painful. The factual sciences begin where common sense begins: with the sensed qualities or properties of things. Consequently, scientific knowledge is really a refinement of common-sense knowledge. Conversely, anything that cannot be sensed through the faculties of the nervous system cannot have the status of fact. *Something* must be perceived before one has stuff at hand for empirical analysis or for incorporation into the structure of scientific knowledge. The soft, yellow, five-inch-long object called " banana " is an object of sensory experience that may become a scientific fact in the full sense of the word. On the other hand, God cannot be a fact because one cannot see, hear, smell, or touch him. An investigator can see amoebae under a microscope or observe a meter register something called electrical current. But neither microscope, telescope, nor radar can register on my nervous system elves, angels, or green dragons. We cannot at this point be called off into a discussion of illusions, hallucinations, and like phenomena with which the psychologist may very well deal.

Our nervous system is somewhat like a complex instrument panel, such as in an airplane cockpit or in a computer control center, on which are registered various things such as " hot," " cold," " swift," " slow," " thick," " pain," " light," " pleasure," and " heaviness." In order for us to have a scientific fact, something must show on the meters and tabulating mechanisms. If none of the meters kicks up, none of the signal lights blazes, or none of the alarms sounds, then there is no fact and nothing with which the scientist can work. Galileo once reported that he saw mountains and valleys on the surface of the moon. He indiscreetly concluded that the moon was not a perfect sphere, as Aristotelian science dictated. His adversaries replied that the heavenly body had to be spherical. Finally, they suggested that the supposed valleys were filled with a transparent stuff, which rounded out the moon to a spherical shape but which Galileo obviously could not see. The unperceivable "transparent stuffs" that men offer as evidence for many of their opinions are spectral evidence. They cannot be seriously considered by the scientist, lest his useful discipline degenerate into witchcraft and his knowledge become an illusion. The scientist must always "see" what he does see, not what he does not see.

2. The scientist must begin with the sensed qualities of first-person experience. He must, however, go beyond this in order to get anything that will be a scientifically useful fact.

Instead of talking about redness, scientists are found talking about 6,500 angstrom units; instead of about swiftness, about 400 miles per hour; instead of about dull sounds, about 60 cycles per second. Before one can have a useful fact, the *qualitative* experience must be subjected to measurement and a *quantity* must be assigned to it. A wire cable conducting electrical current may feel hot. In part, that is a matter of fact. But it is not a very useful fact. One must know *how* hot it is. A tool of some kind — perhaps a calibrated thermocouple — must be used to answer the question, How hot? We can then distinguish with some accuracy the cases in which the electrical systems of our automobiles will ignite from those cases in which we can continue to use the vehicles without danger. It is when the qualitative experience of feeling ill is reduced to some quantitative measures, such as the rate of heartbeat, body temperature, metabolic rate, and bacteria count, that we are getting useful facts about the ill person's condition. Only then can deliberate steps be taken to alleviate or remedy the troublesome condition. The scientist therefore attempts always to define qualitative experiences by some kind of quantitative measures.

When the scientist is able to arrive at a procedure for giving quantitative measures for qualitative experiences, he can generally construct scales for measuring the relative intensities or amounts of a particular experience. Such scales make his data much more useful than they would otherwise be. At 100 degrees centigrade, water (liquid) becomes steam (gas). At 0 degrees centigrade, it becomes ice (solid). Knowledge of this kind helps men effectively to run steam engines, to bathe the baby, to cool their beverages, and to prevent people from breaking their necks on icy sidewalks. If a man constructs even a simple radio circuit, he needs devices to supply and to measure various electromotive forces, such as 5, 6, 60, 100, and 225 volts. In some small, complex machines metal parts 0.543 inches plus or minus 0.005 inches in size are required. Exceedingly sensitive and complicated mechanisms and tools, the clocks, automobiles, refrigerators, thermostats, and electrical mixers we find about us every day, can only be produced when the gross sensory data of human experience are subjected to quantitative measurements.

3. The third characteristic of the scientific fact is *reliability*. Consider a postage stamp. Suppose one day it appears to be one-half inch square. The next day it appears as large as a playing card. The third day it is the size of a pinhead. When it is next observed, it is as large as a desk top. This would be rather indecent and inconsiderate of the stamp, we would all agree. It would certainly thwart a man's attempt to mail a letter, especially if other phenomena, such as writing paper, ink, mail trucks, and locomotives, were similarly subject to such radical changes. The size of that stamp would not be reliable. Even if it always looked blue, felt light, and appeared to be flat, one would not have much of a fact.

There would not be any human knowledge, scarcely any orderly world at all, if sensory qualities and their quantitative measures did not exhibit a degree of reliability. Of course, there actually are small changes in the size of a postage stamp from day to day, or hour to hour, due to changes, say, in temperature and humidity. But repeated measurements of its sides vary only a few thousandths of an inch. If it is repeatedly measured under controlled conditions of temperature and humidity, even less variation appears. It is a reliable phenomenon and therefore a useful one. The property of reliability in part constitutes its factualness. Those who have studied the brand of mathematics known as statistics are acquainted with the many devices used to interpret a collection of varying measures made of a phenomenon.

In order to be a fact that is usable in scientific inquiry, a phenomenon must be reliable. This means that, time after time, under the same conditions, as one or more observers come to the phenomenon, it will yield approximately the same measurement or the same effects.

The three factors mentioned constitute a fact in the scientific sense of the word. Consider a piece of steel, machined in the form of a cube, with edges one-half inch in length. It is a fact because (1) it appears in consciousness as a blue-gray, hard, smooth, . . . object; (2) it can be subject to measurement by, say, a micrometer, so that one can give a quantitative specification for its length, 0.502 inches; (3) time after time as measurements are made under certain fixed conditions, it does not deviate from 0.502 inches by more than one or two thousandths of an inch. Its measured characteristics and its relationships to other phenomena can, therefore, be incorporated into the fund of scientific knowledge. It can be used to build machines that will operate reliably. The example of the steel cube is very simple. On the other hand, when the physicist works with electrical circuits, which are structurally very intricate and where he must concern himself with elements such as resistances, capacitances, and inductances and with phenomena such as current, voltage, and magnetic flux, an adequate and exact specification of fact becomes somewhat more complicated. Furthermore, as one passes from one science to another, the sensory data that have to be subjected to measurement will change considerably. The archaeologist deals with pottery, inscriptions, and masonry; the psychologist attends to reflexes, motivation, and neuroses; the biologist considers photosynthesis, nutrition, and reproduction; and so on. Nevertheless, it is clear that in whatever field scientific work is prosecuted, the scientist is interested in dealing with facts in the sense in which we have defined them.

Another remark about reliability is necessary. It must be emphasized that the term refers simply to the observed repetition, within limits, of the qualitative or quantitative aspects of a phenomenon. One never discovers *why* there is this consistency or stability. Many a devotee of modern science, amazed at the reliability of scientific facts and knowledge, hastily concludes that science explains why this degree of orderliness and consistency appears. Ten thousand measurements of 0.502 inches on the steel cube no more explain why it is 0.502 inches, or remains 0.502 inches, than do three measurements. Ten thousand measurements may be good evidence that the first several measurements were substantially correct. They may even give one greater assurance that the next time the operation is performed the result will be close to 0.502 inches. The extra 9,997 measurements, however, explain nothing. To point out that the reliability of a fact *describes* rather than explains an orderly structure is simply one way of indicating that science is precluded from making metaphysical judgments.

The scientist's insistence on appeal to facts has resulted in his often being deprecated as one committed to a materialistic view of the world and of human life. This criticism has generally been unjustified. Let us consider the matter by looking at a particular issue. There has been, and still is, in some religious quarters much consternation because newer developments in psychology seemed to substantiate a "materialistic view" of man. According to this materialistic view of man, mental operations — for example, rational thought, memory, and imagination — are nothing but subtle physical, chemical, and electrical changes in the nervous system. Behaviorism approximated a position of this kind on the relationship of mind to body. In recent years, an extreme behaviorism has gradually been abandoned as too simple a hypothesis to describe adequately human behavior in all its ramifications. Mind is certainly dependent upon body (they are apparently interdependent aspects of the person), but to say that mental operations depend upon bodily states and changes is different from saying that mental operations are nothing but physical transactions. The qualitative character of imagination, for example, is different from the quantitative data we can gather concerning, say, glandular functions and electrochemical nerve impulses, with which imagination may very well be correlated. Thus the redness of an apple is different from 6,500 angstrom units (its quantitative measure); the vividness, richness, clarity, and progress of images and concepts in consciousness are different from whatever quantitative measures are found for the correlated physical changes in the body.

A slightly more modest doctrine in psychology was quite frequently defended some years ago: epiphenomenalism. It insisted that bodily changes are basic, that mind depends upon body, and that there is no influence of mind on body. According to it, the distinctive qualitative nature of mental operations is admitted: mind is different from body. But mind is not autonomous. Moreover, it cannot, as a cause, produce physical changes. Physical, electrical, and chemical changes in the nervous system or body can produce mental changes, but not vice versa. Mind is not separate from body; nor is it independent of body. This view understandably resulted in much distress among the apologists of the Christian faith, some of whom defended the integrity and distinctiveness of the human soul and believed the soul to be separable from the body as well as to be the initiator of certain types of behavior.

Much of the distress proceeded, however, from a failure to understand the scientist's position. The defender of the faith judged that the scientist was taking an adamant, materialistic position, that is, was proposing and defending, as such, a philosophy that was directly contrary to the received theology. On the contrary, the scientist, wishing to secure facts concerning human behavior, could only easily find observable and measurable phenomena for the construction of knowledge about man by dealing with the physical structure and functioning of the organism. He could not find such facts by taking as his point of departure some prejudice concerning an unperceivable, immeasurable soul. He had to begin where he could observe and measure things. That is, the scientist adopted epiphenomenalism as a *methodological* device, not as an adamant philosophy of human nature or as a metaphysical theory. As a *method* it could be retained if found useful for understanding and predicting human behavior. As a *method* it could also be rejected if found inadequate or unuseful. The intensity of the dispute over this matter and much of the confusion attending it would have abated if men of faith had understood that scientists were not promulgating an anti-Christian message but were using and testing a tool. Epiphenomenalism was a hypothesis used as a tool for inquiry. The psychologist sought facts about human nature, and this hypothesis specified a method by which he could find them. It was expedient. It was useful. These considerations are what count in science. As long as epiphenomenalism retained its hypothetical and methodological status, its retention was justified. Such a scientific approach to human behavior should not give the faithful sleepless nights. Of course, there were some men in psychology who mistakenly defended epiphenomenalism as a philosophy of human nature. To the extent that they did this and failed to recognize a hypothesis as such, they became apostates from science. Their unyielding defense of a false science is as much to be deprecated as utter dogmatism in religion. Any man who closes his mind, whether in science or religion, is neither very scientific nor very religious. He is no longer humble in the presence of truth. He has stopped inquiring, which is the same as committing intellectual suicide. Dogmatism of that kind is the abomination of desolation in both science and religion.

We have used epiphenomenalism as an example of a methodological hypothesis employed to discover facts related to human behavior. There is considerable doubt that it is any longer an adequate tool. For example, it does not seem to be commensurate with the phenomena of suggestion, hysteria, the contextualistic structure of personality, and so on. We are not here defending it as an adequate contemporary hypothesis. The point is that there exist today other scientific hypotheses that have similarly produced distress among religious minds. A proper understanding of the ways in which the scientist probes for facts and for the relations among facts can result in the elimination of that distress.

In the beginning of scientific inquiry is the fact.

Chapter III

What a Fact Is Not

Men who early in life fall in love with science are likely never to recover completely from their undiscerning affection for their first love. They continue to ascribe more virtues to their beloved than she really possesses. Especially those who have not submitted themselves to the disillusioning, disciplining experience of experimental work in a laboratory will remain deceived concerning the absolute perfection of their beloved. But the man who must pit his mind and body against resolute facts in the experimental laboratory finds that while they are quite formidable and disconcerting phenomena, they are not the immutable or absolute data the uninitiated would assume.

A fact is not an absolute but a relative item of experience. Relative to what? This is the question we try partially to answer here in order to complete the definition of a scientific fact. For our purposes, the so-called relativity of a fact can be specified in four ways. These are four ways in which one can state what a fact is not. The significance of all the points to be made here is not generally recognized, even among scientists. Yet if one clearly understands them, he will never confuse science with metaphysics, theology, or the testimonies of faith. As a matter of fact, it is safe to say that when scientists are occasionally found defending some metaphysical theory it is because they have failed to appreciate the relative nature of all factual experience and the scientific descriptions given of it. When the difference between science and metaphysics is clearly understood, men will leave off making an idol of science or offering religious faith as scientific knowledge. While science and religion may be related in certain ways, the respects in which they differ must be clearly defined. This is necessary for the integrity of each. To state what a fact is not — or what the limitations of factual data are — serves to specify certain differences between them.

1. A scientific fact is relative to the human nervous system. This proposition was first clearly and confidently enunciated in modern times by George Berkeley (1685–1753), whose *Three Dialogues Between Hylas and Philonous* ought to be read by all who are interested in the philosophy of science. From a literary point of view the *Dialogues* is a second-rate work; but in spite of its brevity, it is one of the very important works on the theory of knowledge. Berkeley already had his conclusions in mind before he began his inquiries and demonstrations. He set out to disprove materialism, to put atheism to flight, and to make God necessary to the world. He was an exceedingly ambitious man. He tried to rationalize these conclusions by showing that there is no *material* world external to or independent of perceiving minds and the ideas they entertain. We must confess at the outset that the philosopher did not prove what he thought he did, nor did he accomplish his purposes. His discourse is, therefore, great in spite of itself. Nevertheless, we are indebted to him for an ingenious and almost irrefutable analysis of the nature and limits of human perception. It is of great importance for understanding the nature of a scientific fact.

Berkeley showed that men do not perceive objects themselves but percepts, that is, responses in the nervous system (in the mind, to use his term) resulting from stimuli located in an unknown external world. To express the idea in simple terms, let us say that our nervous system is like an opaque veil or drape between our minds and the objects of which we are trying to gain knowledge. We can see on the veil the movements of something brushing against the opposite side (our perceptions), but we never see the thing itself. Because we see only the configurations and movements on the veil, we have no assurance that they are an adequate or true reflection of the structure and functioning of the object behind the veil. When this idea is dressed up in its philosophical finery, it is called the egocentric predicament. Every man is in the predicament of having all of his knowledge distinctively his own. He can never be "here," perceiving the remote object through the media of sensations and perceptions, and also "there," outside his skin, getting a face-to-face view of the object. Thus, he can never discover whether his perceptions present an authentic picture of the object in itself. This egocentric predicament is presumably inescapable. So far as knowledge of ultimate reality goes, every man is shut up inside his skin with a collection of perceptions and ideas whose correctness (in the sense of correspondence with reality) he can never determine.

A parable for this idea may be found in the mechanics of television reception. Our perception of things is somewhat like the reception of visual images on a television receiver. Electromagnetic waves strike the antenna upon the roof. These waves are comparable to the objects that we try to know. Down the antenna lead-in wire the radio waves scurry. When they reach the receiver circuit, the signal is filtered, converted, and amplified. The operations in the receiver circuit are comparable to what occurs to stimuli as they are transmitted through our nervous system. Finally, in one of its converted forms, the signal is propelled through a cathode ray tube and undergoes another metamorphosis, so that on the screen we see trees, airplanes, clocks, and bottles of beer. The final pictures are analogous to our perceptions of what we call "trees," "dogs," and "apples." In all probability, there is as much difference between the tall, green, solid trees we "see" and the real objects behind the veil of the nervous system as there is between the visual images on the television screen and the electromagnetic oscillations shuffling through space and into the antenna network. Man as knower is in the predicament of not being

able to probe beyond the content of his consciousness to the
real objects, because everything he has to work with in consciousness is just as subjective and relative as the percepts
whose objective counterparts he is trying to find. Berkeley hap-
pily concluded that this relativity of perception proved that
only minds and ideas existed. This was, of course, too enthu-
siastic a conclusion. He did prove that men know perceptions

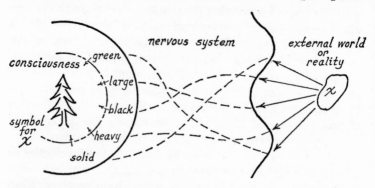

only, not objects in themselves. This is of very great importance for assessing the nature of factual data in science.

Some of the pieces of evidence that Berkeley offered in his
day for this position cannot stand the test of twentieth-century
criticism. But one can draw from modern psychology and biology adequate evidence to confirm his stand. Leaving aside
more technical examples, we can cite some very simple phenomena which indicate the kind of justification that is possible.
For example, dogs evidently hear sounds that are beyond the
perceptual range of the human auditory mechanisms. Two
points spaced one quarter of an inch apart are felt as two when
touched to the fingers, but they are felt as only one when
touched to certain areas of the back. This difference occurs
because of the difference in the concentration of nerve endings
in the two places, and it indicates that our perceptions of unity
or plurality among things are relative to our nervous systems.
Blind and deaf persons, who have lost the use of parts of their

nervous systems, apparently live in a quite different perceptual world from persons who are unimpaired. If the finger tips are sandpapered, surfaces seem rougher than they feel before the operation. A surgical process called prefrontal lobotomy, a cutting away of part of the nerve tissue of the brain, changes radically the perceptual and conceptual world of the patient. In some recent experiments in vision, a subject was provided with lenses that turned his perceptual world upside down and reversed it from left to right. Space relations were thus inverted for him. After several weeks, he was able to perform the normal duties of life without great difficulty.[1] This experiment is not so much to the point at issue as some others, but it is a dramatic demonstration that spatial orientation is purely relative to what we have learned in the past. At a later point, a brief discussion of the special theory of relativity will better show the relativity of perceptions and measurements of extension and duration. Evidences of the kind we have suggested can be multiplied almost without end to demonstrate that the world we see and live in is a characteristically human interpretation of whatever real external world lies beyond our nervous systems and beyond the veil of consciousness.

No one would have doubted that the secondary qualities — color, taste, temperature, sound, etc. — were not in the object beyond the perceiver but in the perceiver's mind or nervous system. Many would have maintained, however, that the primary qualities — extension, motion, solidity, figure, and number — were true representations in the mind of the actual structure and functioning of objects in the external world. Berkeley showed that the arguments that demonstrated the subjectivity of the secondary qualities are just as forceful in the case of the primary qualities. Our perceptions of extension, shape, number, solidity, and motion are peculiarly human interpretations of an unknown external reality. The reddish, solid, sweet spheroid called "apple" is a perceptual creation. It refers to but does not necessarily represent (picture) a structure independent of the perceiver.

A scientific fact, however refined it may be, is part and parcel of this egocentric, perceptual world. It is not an element of the real world outside our skins. It is a feature of the human interpretation of reality. The steel cube that we described earlier is simply a carefully refined segment of this perceptual world. Consequently, a scientific fact is no absolute entity. It is relative to the human nervous system, which is operative in producing a perceptual interpretation of reality. Presumably another kind of animal with a nervous system different from that of man would " see" that steel cube as a quite different sort of object.

Practical men are little concerned with how the world might appear to creatures other than man. For scientific facts, despite this degree of relativity, are reliable. Since they are, scientists can continue to inquire into the world as it appears to man and continue to build rockets and refrigerators. We simply observe in passing that a peculiar conceit is involved in a man's prejudice that the world must really exist as he sees it. It is part of what we may refer to as an anthropocentric view of the world. We shall speak more of it later. At this point we only emphasize that since scientific facts are relative to the human nervous system, it is clear that science gives at best an exact, reliable, and useful description of how the world appears to the human animal. It does not give us an authentic representation of the real world outside our skins. Science, therefore, can never be confused with metaphysics and theology, which do presume to give us pictures or authentic representations of ultimate reality. This lesson needs to be learned as much by scientists as by theologians. At this point, the question remains open as to whether or not the disciplines of metaphysics and theology are actually able to probe successfully into reality. Science surely is precluded from carrying out such projects. This news must quickly reach the ears of those acolytes of science who delude themselves that in science we have a remedy for all the philosophical and religious illnesses of mankind.

It is now clear why one must be suspicious of attempts to

reconcile Genesis or other Biblical texts and science. In essence, Gen., chs. 1 to 11, is theology or metaphysics; it makes assertions, through the device of myth, about what is ultimately real or about God and his ways with men. Science can have nothing positive and definitive to say concerning these matters if it confines itself to facts. If anything is to be said about the truth or validity of the grand assertions of Genesis, it has to be said on some other basis than on that of scientific inquiry into facts and the relations among facts.

2. A scientific fact is also relative to arbitrary standards of measurement. We have become so accustomed to talking in terms of quantitative measures that many of us feel that terms like " foot," " pound," " degree," and " second " designate some kind of absolute entities. These words have natural and inescapable meanings, we feel. The tendency to attribute an absolute character to the quantitative units employed in scientific inquiry is another evidence of the disposition of men to make of science a new metaphysics.

Units of measurement help us to specify only the *relative* sizes of things. To say that a pencil is five inches long and that a side of a room is twenty feet long is simply a rather precise way of saying that the side of the room is forty-eight times as long as the pencil. In all probability, the typical way in which primitive men measured things was by very crudely comparing the sizes of things in their environment. The snake is an arm's length in size. The tree is two men high. Is not this primitive basis of measurement still reflected in certain phrases we use today, such as that which refers to a horse being so many hands high? We also recall that the Biblical cubit was probably the distance from elbow to finger tips. Although we sound more sophisticated today when we talk in terms of millimeters and yards, such quantitative measures are only specifications of the relative sizes of things.

Two sets of units for measurement are in common use in physics, chemistry, and other sciences: the English system of units and the metric system of units. At one time, we measure phenomena in terms of pounds, feet, and seconds; on another occasion, we measure them in terms of grams, centimeters, and seconds. We get just as reliable results in the one case as in the other. We can arbitrarily use the one or the other set of units. Perhaps the only reason for preferring under certain circumstances one set over the other is that the calculations are simpler in one than in the other. There is no question of right or wrong here; the only pertinent questions are those about simplicity and usefulness. Our choice of a set of units makes no difference in the correctness of the results of an experiment.

Standards of measurement are arbitrarily defined. Let us caricaturize the situation to make the point clear. At one time in the past, a group of men came together in the presence of a silver or platinum bar. They placed a scratch on one end and a second scratch on the other end; and they called the distance between the two marks a " yard." They then divided this distance into three equal parts and called each part a " foot." Thereafter, men went about comparing the lengths of things to this bar or to replicas of it, that is, they measured things in yards and feet. It would not have made the slightest difference if they had closed their eyes and blindly inscribed two marks that happened to be as far apart as, say, the height of a telephone pole. This interval could have been called a " beel." They then could have divided the beel into seven hundred equal divisions and called each of these smaller parts a " geel." Each geel could have been divided into three parts, and a third of a geel be known as a " keel." Provided common consent could have been gained for these units, men would then have measured the sizes of things in terms of beels, geels, and keels. We would still be able to build our radar mechanisms and garage apartments. Our computations might be somewhat more arduous, but the results of scientific inquiry and invention would be the same. Things would be unchanged, but our talk about things would have changed.

Thus, when we said that the steel cube was 0.502 inches along an edge, we did not specify any absolute character of the object. We simply gave a very exact specification of its size *relative to* an arbitrary standard that men adopted in order that they could speak without confusion about phenomena in their perceptual world.

3. A scientific fact, with whatever numerous quantitative measures it is described, is relative to the number and nature of the operations performed by men on the qualitative experience from which it arises.

Consider once again that steel cube. As a qualitative experience, it is a small, blue-gray, hard object. A micrometer is applied to it (a first operation) and a report of 0.502 inches on an edge is given. It is put on a scale (a second operation) and a report of 0.56 ounces results. Other more complicated operations may be performed on it, such as are involved in testing the magnetic flux density one can produce in it, determining its resistance to stress, or finding the resistance it offers to the flow of electrical current. For each operation, there is a report of a quantitative measure that specifies some additional characteristic of the cube. As more operations are performed, more data about that cube appear. If some conceivable operation goes unperformed, then one lacks as much data as would be derived from performing it. The factualness of the steel cube, then, is relative to the number of different kinds of operations performed on it. Again we see that the precisely defined fact of science is, in this respect, nothing fixed and absolute. One can also understand part of the reason for the seemingly endless nature of scientific inquiry into even quite familiar objects, such as pieces of metal, trees, salt, sulphur, and rats. As men develop different or more sensitive tools or as they conceive of new operations to perform on an object, they continue their inquiries into it and tabulate the results of their gestures, manipulations, and measuring operations. The fact thus acquires new levels of meaning, more accurate measures, and new relations to other facts.

A well-trained scientist engaged in research on some relatively new or undefined phenomenon is not unlike an infant who stumbles across a new object. In both cases, the meaning of the new phenomenon is *constructed* by recording in memory or on data sheets the results of gestures made toward the novel thing. Consider a young child who, for the first time, directs his attention to an electrical outlet on the wall of a room. Here is something " new." Well, it is relatively new anyway. It is not entirely new, because perhaps he at least senses that the small rectangular plate is similar in shape to some cards with which he plays and that the circular sockets seem to be like coins he has frequently seen about the house. By applying at random eyes, fingers, and tongue, he acquires information about the outlet. These are operations that yield data about the object. Perhaps he then picks up a stray piece of wire and pushes the ends into the small slots and consequently sees fire and hears a crackling sound. If he survives, the novel object is classified as a source of fire and noise. This becomes a part of its factual-ness to him. Later, taking a clue from mother, he plunges the vacuum sweeper plug into the outlet and learns that it is a source of wind. And so on. Layers of meaning are added to the fact as new and more subtle operations are performed on it. He acquires only as much information about it as he derives from the various operations that he performs on it.

Even as an adult, he may never know that this same object also means interesting pictures on an oscilloscope screen, sim-ply because he has not been in a position to perform the requi-site operation. This is, of course, an overly simple description of the construction of the meaning of the fact. But the pro-cedure of the scientist is, functionally speaking, the same as that of the child. The scientist is, however, somewhat more subtle and exact in his maneuvers. As an intelligent, informed, and disciplined inquirer, he engages in extremely intricate op-erations on a source of electrical energy such as we have men-tioned. He uses meters, oscilloscopes, and differential equations as tools of inquiry instead of bare hands, nose, and tongue. Nevertheless, the scientist *constructs* the meanings of facts by performing operations on the qualitative subject matters that have captured his attention. Those meanings are relative to the number of different kinds of operations he performs. In this sense, scientific facts are *made*. That is, perception is not merely a passive transaction but one in which the perceiver is actively at work in constructing meaning. Scientific knowledge, which is built on the relations among facts, is deliberately constructed knowledge of the phenomenal world. Remembering our earlier discussion, we can say that it is a *human construction*. It is, properly speaking, a rationalization of sensory experience.

4. The scientific fact may also be said to be relative in the sense that any quantitative measure given for it is an average value computed from a whole set of varying measures. The measuring operations used on a phenomenon never give, time after time, exactly the same result. There is an irritating arbitrariness about the fact that generally makes it less exact than we expect.

Recall that steel cube again. We said that a micrometer was applied to it and the result was a report that its edge measured 0.502 inches. That judgment is really an *idealization*. What really happens is that we measure the edge, not once, but twenty times, forty times, or perhaps one hundred times. Twenty operations of measurement are recorded thus: 0.502, 0.503, 0.503, 0.5015, 0.503, 0.5025, 0.503, 0.5015, 0.5015, 0.502, 0.502, 0.5025, 0.5015, 0.5025, 0.5015, 0.502, 0.503, 0.503, 0.5025, and 0.502. These numbers are then averaged, and the value of 0.502 inches is reported as the length of the edge of the cube. The final specification of a quantitative measure for a fact in science is generally a simplification and idealization of variable data derived from a series of measuring operations. In part, this is why, in engineering specifications for, say, structural steel or automobile parts, the sizes are given with tolerances. Instead of 0.502 inches, we read 0.502 ± 0.001 inches. The tolerance specification allows for the dispersion of the measured values of the original piece or of subsequent copies of it.

The arithmetic mean, 0.502, of the above set of measurements was used to specify the length of the edge of the cube.

Other averages that are sometimes used, when they are better suited to the purpose of the scientist, are the mode and the median. The mode is the value occurring most frequently in a set of measurements (it would be 0.503 in the above distribution). The median is that value above which and below which half the measurements appear. Although in the example we happen to be using, it would for certain reasons be awkward to use the median, theoretically it would be between 0.502 and 0.5025, that is, presumably 0.50225. A study of statistics reveals other devices for specifying significant features of a set of such measurements. One can characterize the dispersion of the values about the mean, make measurements of the probable error to be expected in a given measurement, characterize the distortion (skewness) of the distribution from a normal curve distribution, and so on.

Let us indicate diagrammatically the point we are making. If each and every measurement on the edge of the steel cube were exactly 0.502 inches, the distribution would look like this:

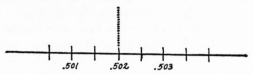

But this very seldom happens. The actual situation is generally something like this:

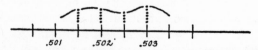

Regardless of whether the variation in measurements is due to inaccuracies in the measuring tool, to faults in the human observer, or to a variation in the thing being measured, the significance of it for our evaluation of scientific method is the same. Again it is clear that the scientific fact is no absolute or fixed element of experience. A quantitative measure for a fact is relative to some distribution of varying numbers resulting from a repeated operation of measurement. This is a general characteristic of the quantitative specifications in the factual sciences. It does not, however, destroy the usefulness of scientific method and knowledge, inasmuch as there is a degree of reliability and stability to the fact and its measures. It does serve to destroy the illusion that in science one is dealing with absolutes or with irrevocable and invariable specifications of reality.

In sum, a scientific fact is relative (1) to the nervous system of the perceiving organism, (2) to the arbitrary standards of measurement employed, (3) to the number of different types of operations performed on the qualitative subject matter, and (4) to a distribution of the varying measures derived from the phenomenon.

What is the significance of these remarks about the nature of a fact? If a fact has the status we have defined, it is obvious that scientific knowledge, which is built on facts, is sharply distinguished from metaphysics and theology. Science deals with carefully quantified, reliable perceptions. It does not deal with what is ultimately real. By its own definition of fact, science can have nothing whatever to do with God or other supernatural entities and forces. It is important to recognize that science is clearly separated from metaphysics and theology by its own criteria, not merely by the declarations of religious persons.

Chapter IV

How Science Inquires

Men of science have their own peculiar and agonizing way of probing into nature. It differs greatly from the method used by religious persons in their search for truth and satisfaction. Here we shall try to characterize and interpret some of the methods science uses for the construction of human knowledge. A description of a portion of the logic of scientific method will help further to define the relations between science and religion.

Facts by themselves have very little meaning. If the human organism were so unfortunate that it could only take note in consciousness of this fact, that fact, and the millionth fact, and could not relate them one to another, there would be no knowledge to speak of. As a matter of fact, there would not be much of a world, in the sense of an orderly arrangement of phenomena. Think of the human mind [2] as a barrel with the bottom removed. One after another, marbles are thrown into the barrel. In they go, and then immediately out again. None is retained and no distinctions are made among them. If the mind simply took note of this and that experience but could not retain or relate experiences, very little knowledge, if any, would result. The mind would entertain in each passing moment an aggregation of chaotic percepts, mysterious in their novelty and isolation.

"Memory" is the term used to denote the ability of the mind to entertain images and ideas over a period of time and in the absence of direct perception of an object. Memory serves as a bottom for the barrel that we mentioned. The marbles are retained after being thrown in. There is now a kind of permanency to the stuff of knowledge and, therefore, something with which to do continuing mental work. The ability to remember is one prerequisite for knowledge.

Retention of images and ideas is not all that is required for the construction of knowledge. Being retained, they have to be related to one another. The mind is able to take note of similarities and differences among the structures and functionings of perceptual things. A small child who has eaten and therefore become familiar to a degree with "hot dogs" and, upon seeing a banana on the table, identifies it as "dog" has begun to note similarities in structures among things in his environment. At a more sophisticated level, the student of mathematics does the same who has learned the meanings of the equations for the ellipse, the hyperbola, and the parabola and, noting points of similarity, moves on in thought to the idea that all the conic sections can be specified by one equation, $Ax^2 + Bxy + Cy^2 + Dx + Ey + F = 0$.

The noting of similarities and the noting of differences are reciprocal processes. To assert that two things differ in some respect presupposes a standard for comparison, which is itself a specification of an element of similarity between the two. Conversely, an assertion of similarity in some respect between two objects presupposes some difference, or else the items are not two but one. Another of the relational facilities of the mind is that of noting relative proximity or remoteness in space and time. Thus, two balls (similar in structure) may be contiguous in space (having their surfaces touching, for example). On the other hand, while similar in structure, they may be at a distance of ten yards or one hundred miles from each other. Eating green apples may be contiguous in time to nausea or remote in time from a marriage ceremony. We are not prepared to list all the relational facilities of the mind or nervous system. We have cited these two, the noting of similarities and contiguities, because they play a very important role in the construction of scientific knowledge. We refer to them here simply to indicate that knowledge is not the bare perception of facts but is built from relations among facts. (These relational facilities of the mind are, of course, already at work in the process of establishing quantitative measures for facts.) When relations among facts are expressed properly in propositions, we then have knowledge in a scientific sense of the word.

If knowledge is an exact and cautious assertion of the relations among facts, we can understand from another point of view the scientist's hesitation to give quick assent to theological doctrines. Many statements concerning the religious life and thought of men intend to relate facts of experience to nonfactual entities (spiritual agents). The scientist cannot, in the first place, accept a term designating an intangible entity as a member of a proposition that, in order to constitute knowledge, must employ terms that denote facts. Secondly, he is inclined to doubt that, in the absence of tangible, public experience of the spiritual agent, one is justified in saying that it bears any relationship to whatever facts of experience one may be speaking about. God does not constitute a part of experience in the same way as do colors, tastes, sounds, images of size, solidity, or speed. To affirm a relationship between two entities requires sensory experience of both, not of just one.

There is one relationship among facts in which the scientist is especially interested. It is the cause-effect relationship. We must comment on it briefly. Everyone knows that the scientist seeks for the causes of events. Everyone knows that the knowledge he thus acquires results in a great degree of control over nature and in an ability to predict with a high degree of reliability what will occur under certain given conditions. That man can control nature by virtue of his knowledge of its ways is evident in the development of the battleship or air-conditioning, the control of disease, the launching of missiles and satellites, and the building of apartment structures. Scientific knowledge also results in an ability to predict. Thus, men can predict the point of impact of a shell fired from an artillery piece, the positions of the planets in their orbits, the specifications for a bridge to span a certain river, and the circuit structure necessary to receive television signals. This control and prediction is possible because scientists have a fund of knowledge about causal connections. What is a cause-effect relationship?

It seems clear that the present scientific understanding of this relationship is based upon the analysis given by David Hume (1711–1776). Hume was a radical empiricist who presented a philosophical rationalization for the inductive and experimental methods of the new science of his day. He first asks what men meant in the past when they used the terms " cause " and " effect." He asserts that they meant three things: (1) the phenomenon called " cause " was contiguous to and immediately preceded the so-called effect in time; (2) the phenomenon called " cause " was contiguous in space to the presumed effect; and (3) there was some necessary, underlying connection between the two phenomena. For example, if a man says that the cutting of a lamp cord carrying current is the cause of the blowing out of the fuses in the electrical circuit in his house, he means three things. The cutting took place an instant before the fuses were blown. The cutting is related closely in spatial categories to the blown fuses (for example, in terms of the wires running eventually to the fuse box). And there is some necessary, underlying connection between the two events that goes beyond the first two matters mentioned. He thinks of this vaguely in terms of a short circuit through the steel cutters, high current in the line, heat, and the melting of metal. In any case, he is sure that the cutting of the cord and the blowing of the fuses were not accidentally conjoined. This is the traditional way of understanding the cause-effect relationship, says Hume. Indeed, it is still the common-sense understanding of it. As a radical empiricist, Hume insists that nothing can be considered knowledge that cannot be traced to sensory impressions. He will apply this test to the threefold definition. The first two points can stand. We can experience and measure contiguities in space and time. But, says Hume, no one ever experiences a necessary connection. Every fragment of sensory evidence one brings forward from a cause-effect situation will deal only with the two objects or events and their spatio-temporal connections. In the example given, everything a man cites as evidence for the cause-effect relationship has to do with wire, wire cutters, fuses, molten metal, heat, shock, and so on — all of which are sensory data connected with the prior phenomenon or the latter. Nowhere does a man get sensory data for the supposed necessary connection. The third item in the traditional specifications for the cause-effect relationship is empirically (scientifically) unjustified. Hume ascribes it to an expectation that arises in the mind as a result of the repeated association of the two phenomena in past experience.

In science, then, the term "cause-effect relationship" refers, according to Hume, merely to a regular conjunction of two phenomena in space and time. That is, the term describes, rather than explains, how two events have been connected in past experience. Let us use another example. We assert, perhaps, that a rise in temperature of 50 degrees centigrade will cause a fifty-foot steel rail to increase in length by five sixteenths of an inch. This causal statement simply means that in the past, once, twice, three times, . . . , or five hundred times, when such beams suffered a temperature rise of 50 degrees centigrade, we observed that as a matter of fact they increased in length by five sixteenths of an inch. This is all that the causal statement means. It is *descriptive* of this limited but regular experience. To talk about underlying connections is superfluous and meaningless. This is what a cause-effect relationship meant to David Hume. In great measure, it is what this relationship means in science today.

This interpretation of causal relations has considerable significance for the nature and competence of scientific method.

1. This understanding of cause-effect relationships reaffirms what was said earlier about scientific method when we spoke

about the nature of fact, namely, that what science does is to describe the world as it appears to man. All scientific theories or laws built upon cause-effect relationships are simply highly refined descriptions of certain aspects of the phenomenal world. All the factual sciences are, properly speaking, descriptive sciences. They may differ from one another in the exactness and reliability of the descriptions they give of their data; but they all do nothing more than describe. In science, there is no explanation in the sense of getting at necessary connections, metaphysical stuffs, or irrevocable and prescriptive laws. Science does not answer the question Why? It only answers the question How?

2. Since cause-effect relationships are descriptive of past experience, and all human experience, by an individual or by a group, is limited, there is no such thing as certainty in the empirical sciences. All scientific knowledge is only more or less probable, depending upon the range and refinement of the factual data upon which it is based. The fact that scientific knowledge is descriptive and probable does not preclude the predictive function to which we referred earlier. A hypothesis based upon extensive observations and experimentation and having, therefore, a high probability factor associated with it can obviously be used with some degree of assurance in prediction. In the example given above, if one is laying rails for a railroad, he will feel a high degree of assurance that from winter to summer the steel rails will expand by a certain calculated amount, and he will consequently leave an expansion gap of appropriate size. Scientific prediction does not require certainty (which it cannot have anyway) but only a high probability concerning the occurrences of the effects when the causal factors appear. It is clear that there is a real exercise of "faith" in scientific prediction.

3. Inasmuch as science is restricted by its own subject matters and methods to description, it cannot legislate in metaphysics and theology. There are men who will make of science a new theology or who will try to use scientific data to warrant

metaphysical or theological propositions. It is clear that all such attempts are ill-conceived and vain. The nature of its methods prevents science from saying anything about the truth of such assertions. This implication of the scientific understanding of cause-effect relationships harmonizes, then, with the results of our earlier analysis of the relativity of scientific facts. Later we shall try to show that the most that can be said about the relations between science and religion on this matter of the warranting of propositions is that no assertions of a sane and sincere religion can contradict the assured results of scientific inquiry into the phenomenal world.

Another topic related to scientific methods ought to be mentioned briefly. The scientist employs certain canons, or principles, of experimental procedure in order to warrant causal statements of the kind we have just described. It is worthwhile discussing some of them as a further introduction to an understanding of science. Let us say first of all that we must overlook some of the canons and omit certain technical details in the ones we do present. We cite three of these rules of experimental procedure in roughly the form in which they were laid down by John Stuart Mill (1806–1873). They are known as (1) the Principle of Agreement, (2) the Principle of Difference, and (3) the Principle of Concomitant Variation.

These three principles of scientific inquiry are supposed to determine warranted statements of causal relationships that escape the errors and deceptions involved in making assertions on the basis of uncritical observation and undisciplined inquiry. The farmers of ancient Canaan were in the habit of pouring consecrated liquids upon their grain fields, accompanying the libations with incantations and chants. The rites were expected to be followed by a hearty growth of grain and a bountiful harvest. They casually and uncritically observed that phenomenon A (the rites) was followed by phenomenon B (growth and harvest). Because their analysis was cursory, they overlooked the exceptions and hastily generalized that the libations and other magical rites, along with the divine powers they summoned, caused the fertility of the fields. Even today in many areas of study and action, people are content to make causal statements on the basis of an uncritical review of the evidence, a resort to nonfactual entities, simple enumeration, and hasty generalization. The prescientific attitude is especially prominent in the cases of men's judgments about social affairs, political matters, and religious phenomena. The scientist's critical and cautious attitude precludes such precipitous judgments. Before he states a causal relationship, the man of science wants to make his observations as wide and as detailed as possible, to consider all the varied circumstances in which the phenomena with which he is concerned will occur, and to be extremely critical in order to avoid erroneous generalizations. Even then, the formulation of the causal relationship is considered by him to be the fabrication of a hypothesis rather than the firm proposal of a final statement.

The canons of inquiry we mentioned are designed to help the scientist to escape the errors of uncritical observation and hasty generalization. The Principle of Agreement is formulated in this way. The relationship of two events, A and B, may be affirmed to be a causal relationship if, in a fixed context, the appearance of A is uniformly followed by the appearance of B. Suppose we have at hand a boxlike chamber, constructed so that we can place some rats in it. It also has a hose attached to it, through which we can inject gas into the chamber. We place some rats in the chamber and subsequently inject gas. The rats die within a few minutes. Once, twice, . . . , and a hundred times, we perform this test. Phenomenon A, the gaseous atmosphere, and phenomenon B, the death of the rats, are without exception conjoined. The Principle of Agreement states that this regular conjunction justifies the assertion of a causal relationship between the two. It is clear that the use of the Principle of Agreement results only in a many-to-one causal law. It determines that A is one of many possible causes of B, or that B is one of many possible effects of A. A causal formula based only on the regular appearance together of two events is not a sufficiently precise formula. One may have to be content with it, however, in certain experimental situations where it is impossible to remove or negate the supposed causal factor.

To supplement the first principle, the Principle of Difference can be applied in many situations. It is expressed this way. The relationship of two events, A and B, may be affirmed as a one-to-one causal relationship, if, in a fixed context, the appearance of A is regularly conjoined with the appearance of B, and the nonappearance of A is regularly conjoined with the nonappearance of B. If, when one institutes the supposed causal factor, the supposed effect occurs, and if, when one withdraws the supposed causal factor, the supposed effect disappears — then the first phenomenon is the cause of the second. Suppose we support an iron bar in a water bath. There is a device at hand for measuring the length of the bar. There are also facilities for raising and lowering the temperature of the water and, therefore, of the iron bar. Now the temperature of the water bath and therefore of the bar is raised. We observe that the bar increases in length by a certain amount. Then we lower the temperature, and the bar decreases in length to its original size. This operation is performed repeatedly, with no exceptions occurring in the way in which the phenomena are related. The Principle of Difference expresses the thought that under such circumstances we are justified in asserting that it was the temperature rise and only the temperature rise that caused the increase in the length of the bar.

These two principles suggest the kind of procedures one must employ in experiment in order to arrive at a causal relationship. In addition to them, a third principle is necessary and useful. Notice that the first two canons allow a statement of a causal relationship only between what we may call gross phenomena; for example, injection of gas into a chamber, death of animal life, rise in temperature, or increase in the length of an iron bar. The scientist is generally interested in more exact statements than those which can be made on the basis of the first two canons. If he is successfully to control and predict natural phenomena, he needs to know, not merely *that* a rise in temperature causes iron to expand, but *how much* of an expansion is caused by a given temperature rise. Otherwise, the business of building bridges and skyscrapers would be a rather haphazard and disastrous process. To the first two principles, therefore, a third is added: the Principle of Concomitant Variation. In simple terms, it is this: two phenomena are concomitantly conjoined (and thus their relationship can be described in some precise mathematical or logical formula), if for every variation in one the other is found to vary according to some constant law. The testing procedures dictated by this canon have to take place in a fixed context or under controlled conditions. If we continue with the example cited earlier, the principle speaks about a situation something like this. The temperature of the water bath and iron bar is varied from 0 to 10 degrees, and we observe that the length of the bar increases 0.001 inch. A temperature rise from 10 to 20 degrees results in an increase of 0.00095 inch. In the third case, for the rise from 20 to 30 degrees, the expansion is 0.0012 inch. We continue in this way until the temperature reaches 100 degrees, and then we lower the temperature in 10-degree steps, noting the correlated contractions of the bar, until we reach the starting point. This set of operations and measurements is performed repeatedly, and the results remain substantially the same. There is a rather constant ratio of increase in the length of the bar to temperature rise, namely, 0.001 inch per 10 degrees. Now we are justified in making a more precise statement about the relationship of temperature rise to increase in length than that the first phenomenon is the cause of the second. We are able to express this causal relationship in a formula:

$$\text{Increase in Length} = 0.001 \frac{(\text{Temperature Rise})}{10}$$

With this precise formula we are in a position to predict and control situations where iron bars are subject to rise in temperature.

We have overlooked many details in this abbreviated description of Mill's principles of inquiry. Our interest here is only in a simple, correct understanding of one aspect of scientific method. It may be valuable to mention some criticisms of these canons. First of all, it is really faulty to state them positively as we have done above. Their real force is better expressed in a negative form:

(1) Nothing can be a cause of an event if it is not, under controlled conditions, regularly conjoined with that event.

(2) Nothing can be the sole cause of an event that, under controlled conditions, is not regularly conjoined with it and that is present in the absence of that event.

(3) No phenomena are concomitantly conjoined if, under controlled conditions, the variations in the phenomena are related by no rational pattern or constant law.

These statements express the real meanings of the principles, which are less than the positive forms given earlier would lead one to believe. What this means is that Mill's canons cannot be used to *establish* the causes of phenomena; they can be used only to *eliminate* with certainty false causes. In other words, they are not methods of discovery or proof. Causal assertions erected on the basis of the canons are, therefore, less than certain.

A second remark may be made. The use of each of the principles presupposes a fixed context or controlled conditions. For example, one would not make much headway in specifying the causal relationship between the volume and pressure of a gas if he were not aware that changes in temperature would affect his measurements (were relevant). In other words, the use of the principles assumes that a fund of knowledge has been acquired so that the experimenter knows to some extent what is relevant and what is irrelevant to his problem. Only then can he control the factors in the experimental situation in such a way as to apply these principles and proceed to the formulation of hypotheses. Where judgments of relevance have not been made or cannot be made, the scientist must proceed by trial and error until a sufficiently great number of unfortunate experiences teaches him what is relevant and what is irrelevant to the problem with which he is working. The two remarks we have made suggest that there is a large element of shrewd guesswork in inductive thinking. Bertrand Russell once observed that scientific induction seemed to be either disguised deduction or a method of making informed guesses. But more of this anon.

There is a sounder understanding of modern scientific method than is suggested by Mill's canons. We can mention it only briefly here. According to this contemporary view, the scientist (1) makes certain observations and measurements and brings to them, and interprets them by, a set of abstract concepts (for example, the elliptical form for observations on the orbits of planets); (2) makes logical and mathematical deductions from the mathematical formulations of these concepts; and (3) finally makes observations to see whether or not his deductions (predictions) are corroborated by facts. If the deductions from the hypotheses are corroborated, they are continued in use; otherwise, they are abandoned or revised. Within the context of this understanding of scientific methodology, a causal relation is any relation that lends itself to this sort of formulation and has predictive value. Scientific method is thus interpreted as chiefly a deductive process rather than an inductive one. An accent is placed on the fact that the human mind creates and brings to factual data abstract concepts.

This theory of scientific method also entails the important ideas that (1) one can reject a hypothesis with certainty (if its deduced consequences are not corroborated), and (2) one can never establish a hypothesis or causal relationship with certainty (for generalization and prediction are always related to a limited number of cases). Verification among the factual sciences never establishes a law with certainty. Moreover, any theory of methodology among the factual sciences stumbles over the problem of induction by simple enumeration, which in simple terms is the question as to when, in enumerating black crows, we are justified in asserting, " All crows are black." This problem is inescapable in modern science because the formulations of laws are generally given in strictly universal propositions (mathematical formulas), while those formulations are supposed to be based on observations and measurements of factual data that are almost always limited. There is no logically secure way from existential assertions about factual data to universal statements about all cases of a given kind of data. It is logically fallacious to argue that since 100,000 cases of black crows have occurred (without exception), therefore all crows are black. The problem of induction unmasks the conceit of certainty in science. We shall return briefly to this topic in Chapter XII.

We have reviewed quickly some of the criteria for scientific knowledge and some of the canons of procedure for establishing such knowledge. Knowledge among the factual sciences is clearly less than certain. Let us state one of the chief lessons we have learned with respect to the relations between science and religion. It is that science is prohibited by its very subject matters and methods from making metaphysical judgments and that the philosopher and theologian can make no positive use of scientific knowledge to justify metaphysical and religious ideas or assertions. Our analysis of the nature of fact would have been sufficient to establish this. But now we observe, in addition, that the scientific understandings of causal relationships as regular conjunctions of facts and as mathematical formulas with predictive value do not give any help in arriving at metaphysical entities or connections. As a matter of fact, they too emphasize that there is a sharp line of demarcation between science and metaphysical speculation.

What does the scientist do, or what does he arrive at? He merely describes with great accuracy the relationships of facts to one another in the perceptual world. Moreover, his principles of inquiry are ones that guide the process of relating phenomena to one another; they do not lead him beyond perceptual data. Scientific knowledge, then, is simply a highly articulated and accurate description of the human interpretation of reality. It is exceedingly useful in building houses, detecting aircraft by radar, constructing guided missiles, and manufacturing automobiles. For these benefits all men should be grateful and should feel obliged to defend the integrity of science. Science cannot, however, prescribe in the areas of religion and metaphysics.

Chapter V

What Science Assumes

Some unenlightened partisans of science talk as if science is the one field in which there are no assumptions. The idea that science has no postulates or axioms, or that in it nothing goes unproved, infests many minds. The highest conceit in any field — scientific, religious, or otherwise — is the assumption that there are no assumptions. The scientist does typically employ methods that are based on certain unproved presuppositions. A discussion of some of them may help further to lay bare the skeleton of scientific methodology.

If we call to mind our study of plane geometry (Euclidean geometry), we will remember that at the very outset of this discipline certain definitions, axioms, and postulates were given. A line and a point, for example, were defined. Definitions are arbitrary stipulations of the ways in which terms are to be used. That is, by them the meanings of the terms are fixed. Under the heading of axioms, we read such things as "The whole is equal to the sum of its parts" and "Equals added to equals yields equals." Axioms are not definitions but self-evident truths (so-called). They are assertions that are self-authenticating: every normal mind recognizes immediately and clearly their truth. A postulate is not a stipulation of meaning or a self-evident truth. It is an assertion assumed to be true; that is, it is a basic assumption. It cannot be proved, but it must be used in order to demonstrate other propositions. The famous Euclidean postulate is the one about there existing

only one line parallel to a given line through a point external
to the latter. This assumption has to be used in order to go on
to further demonstrations in the Euclidean system about the
properties of circles, triangles, rectangles, and other forms.
Axioms and postulates are not demonstrated by any rational
or empirical procedures of argument or inquiry. They are
primitive propositions that are needed to prove other assertions.
Mathematicians today do not distinguish between axioms and
postulates. All unproved assertions in a system are postulates.
There are no self-evident truths. We cannot, however, enter
into a discussion of this issue here.

What are the basic postulates employed in scientific inquiry?

One fundamental assumption upon which scientific inquiry
proceeds is that the phenomenal world is *at least in part* an
orderly scheme of affairs (or reflects an orderly scheme of affairs). The world is not completely disjointed and awry. The
scientist assumes that there are certain patterns among events
or that there is a certain degree of rational structure in the
world. The use of this axiom is reflected in his conception of a
cause-effect relationship as a regular conjunction of two phenomena and in his use of prediction. It is also exhibited in the
statements of the three canons of inquiry that we discussed
earlier. The idea of regular conjunction would never be used
in the statement of the three principles of inquiry except on
the basis of this assumption. Moreover, the axiom seems to find
some justification in the reliability of factual data. When we
say that the idea that the world is in part an orderly structure
is a postulate or axiom, we do not mean that there is no presumptive evidence for it. We simply mean that, as a general
proposition, it cannot be proved. The recognition of innumerable cases of reliability in the appearance of quantitative measures for facts is, for example, a piece of presumptive evidence
for the continued use of this postulate, although proof in the
strict sense of the word is impossible.

A second postulate of scientific method is that every phenomenon in the world is subject to causal explanation (descrip-

tion). This assumption is clearly displayed in the scientist's persistent inquiry for the causes of events whose connections with other events are as yet inadequately described. If he did not employ this assumption, scientific inquiry would be brought to a halt. For our purposes, the postulate can be stated in this way: every event has a cause and the same cause is followed by the same effect. The use of this postulate does not necessarily mean that the world is considered to be a unified, causal scheme. It may only express the thought that nature is a matrix of many different groups of causal sequences, rather loosely connected with one another, into one of which any particular phenomenon must fall.

A third postulate of science is commonly known as the doctrine of the uniformity of nature. This assumption goes beyond the first one cited. Here the idea is that one has a "right" to expect that the kinds of conjunctions and connections discovered among phenomena in past experience will also obtain in the future. Of course, if one has thoroughly absorbed Hume's criticism of cause-effect relationships, this expectation is diluted with doubt. In other words, the scientist's expectation is expressed in a probable judgment rather than a certain one. But, even if the judgment is a probable one, it rests upon a "faith" in this assumption. The extensive use of prediction in science is based on this axiom. Were it not taken for granted, predictive inferences would not occur. For example, on the basis of observations of the orbital positions of Saturn, we predict that the planet will be at a certain point in the celestial sphere on April 20, 1970. The confidence we have in the fulfillment of the prediction and the commitments we make on the basis of it are expressions of our "faith" in the axiom of predictive uniformity.

Scientific inquiry proceeds upon a "faith" in such postulates. They are postulates, because they cannot be proved. Nevertheless, they must be used to prosecute scientific work. The scientist's confidence in them and his use of them are expressions of a kind of "faith," an "evidence of things not seen."

They are continued in use because of men's experience of repeatedly successful prediction. They are, therefore, not speculative assertions. Repeated experience, because it is limited and always will be limited, cannot, however, constitute conclusive proof. Upon such postulates the whole superstructure of scientific inquiry and knowledge rests. Just as the massive superstructure of Euclidean geometry rests upon a small base of axioms and postulates, so modern science does also. Valid non-Euclidean geometries have been developed on the basis of postulates other than those used in the Euclidean system. Presumably, other valid ways of dealing with the phenomenal world can be developed than those employed in the factual sciences. This is a way of expressing hope that there may be a valid and useful religious way of dealing with the world that would employ its own distinctive postulates. The fact that science is precluded from metaphysics keeps the way open for this possibility to be realized.

Galilei-Newtonian science used another assumption that should be described: a representative theory of knowledge is adequate or valid. This assumption lies at the heart of that classical system of science but probably can be discarded nowadays. Nevertheless, most men, including many men of science, have not yet realized that it is no longer indispensable. At least they continue to talk and to act as if they were exercising "faith" in it. This is one reason why we must mention it here. Some new developments in physics and chemistry which show that certain principles of the Galilei-Newtonian science are limited cases of more general hypotheses indicate that the assumption to which we refer is not necessary and is, as a matter of fact, controverted in some cases. What does this assumption mean? It means that men assume that certain perceptions or ideas that they have of the extension, solidity, motion, and shape of things accurately represent (picture) the structure and functioning of those things in the external world, independent of their perceptions. Men have long been aware that some perceptions, such as those of color, taste, smell, and sound, were not in the objects themselves, but were generated inside their own skins. The redness and sweetness are not in the apple as an external object but in the perceiver's response to the object. The shrillness of the whistle is our reaction to stimuli from outside our skins. Under the influence of the Galilei-Newtonian science, however, men still held to the assumption that our ideas of extension, solidity, figure, number, and motion were true mental pictures of the state of affairs in

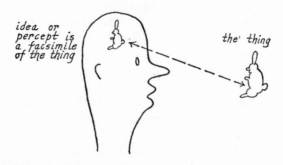

the external world. This axiom seemed to be fortified by the fact that the concepts of absolute space and absolute time appeared to be necessary foundations for Newtonian mechanics. There were frameworks of space and time existing external to and independent of the human mind or perceptual mechanisms. The idea that the human mind takes accurate and reliable "photographs" of reality (in some respects) is what is meant by a representative theory of knowledge. Certain ideas are thought to be facsimiles of things beyond the mind or nervous system.

Our earlier sketch of Berkeley's criticism of perception showed that this theory of knowledge must be called into question. In his *Critique of Pure Reason* and *Prolegomena to Any Future Metaphysics,* Immanuel Kant (1724–1804) helped further to undeceive men concerning this assumption.

From our discussions of the nature of fact and of the egocentric predicament, it is clear that a representative theory of

knowledge must be abandoned. The so-called primary qualities (extension, figure, motion, number, and solidity), to which
John Locke (1632–1704) gave a different status from that of
the secondary qualities (color, sound, etc.), are no more representative of things in themselves than are the latter. Berkeley
showed this. Moreover, this theory of knowledge is not necessary to a proper understanding and prosecution of scientific
inquiry; for the scientist is, according to the canons described
earlier, confined to describing accurately the world as it appears to men. He does not need metaphysical knowledge. He
does not want it, and he cannot use it.

Furthermore, the theory of the relativity of space and time
indicates that extension and duration are not absolute categories, independent of the perceiver. Space-time measurements
are dependent upon the position, motion, and perspective of
the observer and upon his perceptions of the indicators of his
measuring instruments (scales and clocks). There are no such
things as absolute space and time. With the abandonment of
these classical concepts, one of the chief reasons for defending
a representative theory of knowledge disappeared. All that is
required for scientific inquiry is the public availability and use
of standards of measurement in the same way to relate phenomena in the perceptual worlds of human inquirers. We remark in passing that Newton's own scientific arguments for
absolute space and absolute time have been shown to be
faulty, and it has been made clear that these ideas were metaphysical and theological prejudices imported into science. For
Newton, absolute space was the "sensorium" of God. The
theological ideas of the omnipresence and eternity of God
were lurking behind his views on space and time. Finally, recent work in atomic physics indicates that men can speak accurately and usefully about their world in such terms as neu-
trons, electrons, quanta of energy, and electromagnetic fields.
This shows, from another point of view, that the assumption
that ideas of extension, figure, or solidity are valid representations of the external world is unjustified. If one could talk re-

liably, accurately, and usefully only with these gross categories, the assumption might be able to stand with strength. The fact that other categories are just as useful and reliable, if not more so, calls the axiom into question. We do not mean to suggest, however, that these modern categories are themselves representations of things in themselves. They are simply the latest, most useful conceptual shorthand for describing the phenomenal world.

The use of a representative theory of knowledge was a subtle way of smuggling metaphysical commitments into physics. The deception has been thoroughly unmasked, although the news of it is not yet generally known. Once again we see that the very subject matters and methods of science are such as to oust from its quarters any metaphysical assertions, even though they may be disguised in garments tailored by Newton.

In the argument thus far, have we not brought ourselves to the brink of an absurdity? We have agreed with Berkeley that our percepts and ideas (primary and secondary) are relative to the human nervous system. The last fortresses of the objective validity of our ideas were the concepts of time and space (and therefore of motion). The classical contention about their objectivity and absoluteness is not only refuted by Berkeley and Kant but also by the theory of relativity. There is apparently no knowledge of " objective reality " or " ultimate reality." There is no escape from the egocentric predicament. Should we conclude, then, that there is no external world? Are we forced, not merely into agnosticism, but also into solipsism, the idea that I alone exist and that the world is but my grand dream? Frankly, there is no sure reply to this question. The fact that there is no certain response makes a brief discussion of the issue relevant to our present topic, the unproved propositions of science.

We first note that even those who think they have argued themselves into utter skepticism or solipsism do not (cannot) act as if they were suspending judgment on every issue or as if they alone existed. The scientific perspective on knowledge dictates that there can be no certain answer to the question we have posed, for it raises a metaphysical issue. Although the tool of reason is impotent at this point, there seems to be in us a kind of animal faith more basic than reason that moves us to decision and drives us to act *as if* other minds and things existed in an external world. Here is a preliminary clue to the correctness of a position we shall later advance, namely, that while man is rational he is not essentially rational. Reason is a useful tool of the organism, but it is only a tool. For the present we simply remark that where reason cannot persuade us concerning an external world, some irrepressible animal faith causes us to make the bet in the absence of conclusive evidence.

The content of our first-person experience cannot provide conclusive evidence for the existence of an external world. On this score we must agree with David Hume. But, are there some clues in our perceptual world that indicate that the animal faith to which we refer is justified?

1. The reliability of scientific facts reinforces our belief in a consistent structure of some kind in the external world. Even if our percepts or ideas are not facsimiles of real things — even if they are radically different in structure from any such real things — the continuity and coherence of their occurrences are presumptive evidence for some persevering external structure. Morning after morning, upon awakening, the bedroom appears to have the same basic structure and arrangement of parts. Year after year, the topography and the relations of streets, buildings, and walks at Randolph Street and Michigan Boulevard in Chicago remain the same. Experience of this kind prompts the belief that behind the veil of perception there is a continuing structure. This is, however, clearly a matter of exercising "faith."

2. The perceptions I call "my body" (which do feel more directly connected with my consciousness than my perceptions of the arms and legs of others) stand in specific and consistent relations to other parts of my perceptual world. The

consistency of perspective relations is an example.

3. Not only is my body consistently and reliably related to other parts of the phenomenal world, but different things in this world are consistently and coherently related to one another. Temperature rise rather regularly results in the expansion of metal bars; rainfall is generally connected with the healthy growth of crops; electrical current in a wire coiled about an iron bar almost always produces a magnetic field in and about the bar. However subjective the qualities and quantities are to which we refer, the consistency or reliability of the relations among perceptual things seems to be partly rooted in something more than subjective factors. This is, however, not at all certain.

4. The maintenance of certain relations between other parts of my world and my body (in terms, say, of oxygen intake, food consumption, distance from destructive processes, and so on) is necessary for the health or continued existence of my body and my self.

Other evidences of this kind may be cited. They do not disprove Berkeley's contentions about perception or loose the binding power of the egocentric predicament. The epistemological work of Berkeley and Hume did not disprove the existence of an external world. It called its existence into question. Reason cannot settle the matter. Furthermore, the clues of which we just spoke do not indicate a firm answer. They are simply presumptive evidence for the continued use of the axiom that an external world exists. They represent a pragmatic justification for our animal faith. Science and common sense employ the assumption of an external world — thus they make a common venture by " faith."

In the formulation of scientific hypotheses and the relating of hypotheses or theories to one another, we encounter another procedure of axiomatic character. This is the tendency in science to seek for more general, unifying concepts and hypotheses which reconcile and relate specific, limited, and supposedly independent ideas and laws. There is an incessant striving for unity and simplicity in scientific thought. An example will serve to illustrate the point. In the astronomy of Copernicus (1473–1543), it was still thought (as in the Ptolemaic astronomy) that the basic pattern of motion for planetary bodies was circular. Nevertheless, it was clear that the planets did not describe simple circles in their movements about the sun. The paths of these bodies could, however, be adequately described by a combination of circular motions. This composite circular motion was the epicycle. It is the path of a point on a circle, which in turn moves on the circumference of another circle.

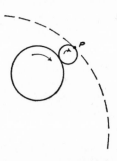

When this description is adopted, it becomes clear that each planet has its own peculiar and complex epicyclical law. We are thus confronted by a multiplicity of laws for the description of planetary motions. One of Johann Kepler's (1571–1630) contributions to astronomy was the formulation of three new laws of motion for the planets. These were: (1) the planets move in ellipses about the sun at one focus; (2) the radius vector from planet to sun sweeps out equal areas in equal intervals of time; (3) the cube of the mean distance from planet to sun is in a constant ratio to the square of the period of its travel in its orbit. The pattern of planetary movements, which was before described by a multiplicity of laws, is now described by only three. This movement in scientific descriptions from the many to the one is a general characteristic of scientific inquiry. The drive to fewer, simpler, and more general formulations is displayed also in the fashioning of a universal law of gravitation, an atomic theory, an electromagnetic field theory, and a single description for gravitational and electromagnetic fields.

Scientific formulations are ranked and ordered in a hierarchy, and there is a constant endeavor to step upward to fewer but more general theories. There is, in short, a drive to monism in scientific thinking. The logical end of scientific descriptions is to comprehend all experience and all subsidiary laws under one, most general but conceptually simple, law or hypothesis. From this grand hypothesis, we expect to predict future occurrences and to deduce all subsidiary laws. Here, then, is another axiom of science: the simpler yet more general descriptive formulations are the more useful and adequate. Traditionally, this assumption is known as the law of parsimony, or " Occam's razor."

The law of parsimony says that if two or more scientific hypotheses are equally adequate descriptions of the factual data at hand, one should choose the simplest. This criterion is not, however, so clear and unambiguous as it seems at first glance. The reason is that there are different kinds of simplicity. The sort of simplicity appealed to in the example above was numerical or conceptual simplicity — one should adopt three laws in preference to twenty-five laws, or he should exercise his option in favor of one law rather than three. We cannot enter into a discussion of the different sorts of simplicity. In order to indicate, however, that the postulate of simplicity in scientific descriptions is ambiguous, we remark that there are aesthetic, transcriptional, conceptual, deductive or predictive, and postulational simplicities. Each is important in its own way. Which one is invoked by appeal to the law of parsimony depends upon the peculiar scientific problem and purpose at hand.

Science is impelled toward unity in descriptive formulations. It hopes to comprehend the phenomenal world under one, universal formula. Is this not precisely what the idea of God means for men of religious faith? The idea of deity is the single concept, under the organizing influence of which the religious person sees meaning and unity in the complex and intricate world in which he lives. The logical function of the idea of God is the same as that of the hypotheses produced in the drive toward unity in scientific formulations. Both science and religion are human inquiries directed to the end of understanding the world. Both exhibit a common logical function in their processes of inquiry, attempting to comprehend the world under one, unifying concept. Just as scientific formulations are rationalizations of human experience, so also the theological formulation termed " God " is a rationalization of human experience. Both science and religion introduce order into the world at the level of conceptualization. One may prefer the scientific rationalization; another may prefer the theological one. We are not concerned at this point with the questions of preference, usefulness, or precision in thought. The logical intent of both is the same. Just as scientific formulations are hypotheses that direct further inquiry, so the idea of God is for religious persons a most general hypothesis that serves to direct their further inquiries and conduct. The retention of scientific hypotheses is based upon their usefulness. The question of the usefulness of the theological hypothesis will be discussed at a later point.

We have characterized some of the assumptions of scientific inquiry. Now let us say a few words about the purpose of science. Its purpose is to understand and control the world in order to turn nature's resources to the satisfaction of human wants. This is a characteristically modern statement of the goal of science. The history of science runs far back in Western history to the pre-Socratic scientists and philosophers. Those ancient inquirers who proposed that all things were made of water, fire, or various states of condensation or rarefaction of air particles, were formulating the first science as well as the first philosophy. From their day up until relatively recent times, men conceived science chiefly as a matter of *under-standing* nature. They had little vision of scientific inquiry as a tool for *manipulating* and *controlling* nature. Even in the cases of Copernicus, Galileo, and Kepler, who began to lay the foundations for modern science, the accent was on under-standing nature and expressing that understanding in mathe-matical language.

Francis Bacon (1561–1626) was one of the first scientists to adopt an inductive and experimental method. In his work, for perhaps the first time, we find expressed clearly the idea that it is the essence of an authentic and useful scientific method to control and manipulate the world. This interpretation of sci-ence took hold in the minds of men slowly. Even in the classi-cal formulation of the new science by Isaac Newton (1642–1727), the emphasis is not on experimentation and manipula-tion, but on observations, correlation of data, and an adequate mathematical description of data. The interpretation of science as essentially understanding was commensurate with the rep-resentative theory of knowledge that, by and large, held the field. As we suggested earlier, this theory of knowledge was stated in a clear form by John Locke, who insisted that the hu-man mind came into the world a blank tablet and that knowl-edge resulted from impressions made upon this sensitive instrument by stimuli from the external world. Locke's formu-lation was a philosophical rationalization of the idea that the purpose of science is chiefly to understand nature.

This view was held by almost every philosopher and scien-tist until the nineteenth century. One of the curious places in which we find the idea expressed that the perceiver is sig-nificantly active in the process of knowing is in the works of Karl Marx (1818–1883), although this revolutionist can scarcely be called a scientist. For him, sensation is not a passive experience; it is one in which the knower is active and in which he manipulates the phenomenal world. We know as a result of manipulating things. The task of the scientist is to alter the world, not merely to understand it. Truth is not passively received. It is produced by the knower. Since the nineteenth century, this interpretation of scientific knowing has prevailed in almost all quarters. It has been found to be justified in terms of the rapid expansion of scientific knowledge through experimentation and in terms of the startling and creative results of such manipulative inquiry. Extremely rapid progress in engineering fields and in technology also bears out the adequacy of this pragmatic interpretation of science. The purpose of science is to understand the world and, by this understanding, to modify and manipulate it to human advantage. As a matter of fact, the understanding itself comes from manipulation.

The idea that science can control or manipulate things in nature is closely connected with the thought that it can predict with some degree of assurance the occurrence of events under certain conditions. As we observed earlier, this predictive function is based upon the assumption of the uniformity of nature. If the phenomenal world is in some measure an orderly domain and if the human knower can manipulate things in it, then prediction is possible. Scientific predictions are made on the basis of hypotheses. Logically, they are expressible in the hypothetical inference, if p, then q. If radium disintegrates in proportion to the mass present, then half its mass will be disintegrated in 1,580 years. If the orbits of planets are elliptical, then they will travel with greater velocity in their paths as they round the sun than they will near the ends of the minor axes of their orbits. If radio waves travel with a finite velocity, then we can measure the time interval between the transmission of a signal from earth and its reflection back to earth from the moon. The " if " part of such inferences is called the " antecedent." It expresses a hypothesis. The consequent, the " then " part, gives the prediction made on the basis of the hypothesis. Granting that the inference holds, if the hypothesis is true, then the prediction must be true. If the prediction is unfulfilled (false), then the hypothesis is proved false in the form in which it was stated in the antecedent. All prediction in science employs the logical form of the hypothetical inference. The assurance one has in his prediction is proportional to how well the hypothesis has been justified by experience and experiment. The logical character of predictive inferences indicates, in another way, the tentative character of scientific judgments. The mathematical formulation of a law, which appears as the hypothesis in the inference, generally goes beyond the limited justification there is for it in experience. Prediction from hypotheses is thus an expression of "faith" in the hypotheses and involves the risk that comes with acting on a probable judgment.

Some may object that what we have just said about the tentativeness of scientific formulations is not right, for scientific hypotheses are verified. What is verification? Verification is another distinctive feature of modern science. The science of Aristotle (384–322 B.C.) and of the Western world generally up until the time of Galileo and Newton appreciated very little, if at all, the necessity of what we call verification. Premodern scientists did not feel that it was necessary to check up on the results of their deductions from basic axioms or postulates. Roughly speaking, verification is simply a matter of checking the scientific hypothesis or predictions from it against the facts encountered subsequent to its formulation. In other words, verification refers to an attempt to corroborate the hypothesis by appeal to factual data. If predictions from a hypothesis are fulfilled, one says that the hypothesis is verified or corroborated. If the element radon disintegrates in proportion to the mass present, then half its mass will be left after 3.85 days. In many cases, it is observed that after 3.85 days, half the mass of the element remains. We judge, therefore, that the hypothesis expressed in the antecedent has been justified. This is what is meant by verification.

The logical pattern of argument used in verification is this: if p, then q; and q; therefore, p. This is clearly an invalid form of argument (the fallacy of affirming the consequent). Verification in the empirical sciences typically employs an inference that is logically fallacious. This means that a scientific hypothesis cannot be established with certainty. On the other hand, it can be rejected with logical security: if p, then q; and not-q; therefore, not-p. If the predictions made from a hypothesis are not fulfilled or are controverted by facts, the hypothesis as stated is false. Scientific hypotheses can always be certainly rejected, but they can never be certainly proved. Nature always answers clearly and loudly, " No," but it only inaudibly utters, "Yes." There is no escape from this difficulty. All scientific descriptions are, therefore, tentative or probable. This does not mean, however, that the procedure of verification is completely unwarranted. If predictions continue to be fulfilled, we at least feel justified in continuing the hypothesis in use. Scientific hypotheses in general have pragmatic value; they are not expressions of certain or absolute truths. Either they work or they do not work. This is what is important as far as the methods and purposes of science are concerned.

Chapter VI

Logic and Mathematics

In John's interpretation of Jesus' mission, the writer has the Nazarene say to Pilate: "For this I was born, and for this I have come into the world, to bear witness to the truth. Every one who is of the truth hears my voice." Pilate answered, "What is truth?" The procurator's reply was probably more an epithet than a real question; but the question expressed in his reply has confounded philosophers and scientists in every century. It will probably continue to perplex them. It would perhaps be a tragedy if men were ever able definitively to answer that question. Were a final response given, human inquiry would be at an end. And with the cessation of inquiry, the process of living would come to a grinding halt. Living is at heart a process of inquiry for the solution of problems. It is entirely appropriate that the inquiries of a finite creature should be incessant, that a final answer to the question of truth should never be given, and that even scientific formulations of knowledge are always tentative and probable.

The word "truth" means different things in different areas of inquiry, and it means different things to different men. At this point, we want to describe what truth means in science and what the difference is between validity and truth.

The distinction between truth and validity is one that corresponds to the difference between the factual and the formal sciences. Thus far, almost all our discussion has been about the factual sciences. They have for their basic subject matter factual data. They are inductive in procedure, beginning with observations and measurements of facts and their relationships and proceeding to the formulation of hypotheses that are descriptive of the phenomenal world. In these sciences hypotheses are checked against facts to assure that the knowledge expressed in them is warranted.

Mathematics and logic, on the other hand, are formal sciences. They presume to lay down rules that govern correct thinking or argument generally. Their basic subject matter is ideas (abstract concepts), not facts. They employ a deductive method, which means that they proceed by relating abstract ideas to one another and by drawing out the detailed meanings or implications of such ideas. In the domain of the factual sciences, truth refers roughly to the correspondence of our assertions to the facts. "Validity" is the term used in the formal sciences to designate the idea that concepts and assertions are combined correctly, whether or not they are true.

The distinction between truth and validity can best be presented by the use of several examples. First, consider these two arguments:

CASE 1

All human beings are mammalian;
all Caucasians are human beings;
hence, all Caucasians are mammalian.

CASE 2

All anthropoids are rational;
all cheetahs are anthropoids;
hence, all cheetahs are rational.

In Case 1, each of the propositions taken by itself is true, that is, it corresponds to the facts. There is, however, another aspect of the argument that is important. It is the way in which the classes referred to are connected to one another. The class human beings is included in the class mammal, and the class Caucasian is included in the class human being. The class relationships are such that the conclusion is necessarily given, namely, that the class Caucasian is included in the class mammal. This conclusion is forced by the class relationships themselves, independent of the specific content of the classes. This sort of logical structure in an argument is called "validity."

Now notice Case 2. If one considers each proposition by itself and asks if it is in accord with the facts, he will probably judge each false. But the logical form of this argument is the same as that of the first. Observe the diagrams of the class structures. The conclusion of the second argument is necessitated in the same way as that of the first one. Both arguments are valid, even though in the first case each proposition is true and in the second case each proposition is false. The logical form of both is:

$$\text{All } Y \text{ is } Z;$$
$$\text{all } X \text{ is } Y;$$
$$\overline{\text{hence, all } X \text{ is } Z.}$$

Any argument structured in this way is a valid argument. This means that if true premises are supplied, a true conclusion must follow.

In order to relate this matter to what we were saying earlier about the hypothetical proposition, notice that the argument can be cast into this form: if all Y is Z, and all X is Y, then all X is Z. If the antecedent is true, the consequent must be true (this is what the hypothetical inference means). We have, then, a very simple illustration of the fact that the scientist, in his formulation of hypotheses and his use of them in prediction, depends upon the logical binding force of the hypothetical inference. This suggests that argument in the factual sciences is simply one application of argument in general. Logic is the science that studies the patterns of correct argument. Thinking and argument in the factual sciences therefore presuppose the categories and principles of formal logic. In those sciences, the scientific knower casts the specific factual data that confront him into logical structures of abstract ideas and arguments. The scientist brings ideas to his data in order to interpret them and, therefore, to give them meaning. As a matter of fact, we may interpret the factual sciences as being engaged in the attempt to make logical thought applicable to the phenomenal world. This bears out, from another point of view, our earlier contention that the knower constructs knowledge. He imposes certain logical structures or certain patterns of order upon the phenomenal data presented to him. In science man makes for himself an orderly world.

The two arguments given earlier were valid. Let us contrast to them two cases of invalid inference.

CASE 3
No vegetable is animal;
all vegetable is living being;
hence, all animal is living being.

CASE 4
No kangaroo is mammal;
all kangaroo is nonsentient;
hence, all mammal is nonsentient.

The form of both these arguments is: no A is B; all A is C; therefore, all B is C. The evidence that A is included is C and that A is excluded from B forces no conclusion concerning the relationship between B and C. Class C may include B or exclude B, on the basis of the evidence presented in the premises. This form of argument is invalid; no one conclusion is necessitated by the evidence. Anyone who argues in this fashion is said to make an invalid inference. This judgment about the

correctness of the argument form is independent of the fact
that every statement in Case 3 is true and every one in Case 4
is false.

The forms of argument based upon the hypothetical inference are, as we have suggested, of great importance for sci-

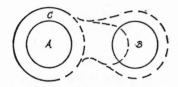

ence, since that inference is indispensable for argument and
prediction. The inference is also used to express causal relationships. When it is so used, the logical form is: if the cause,
then the effect. The if-then assertion states that the antecedent
is *one* condition for the occurrence of the effect expressed in
the consequent. It does not say that the condition stated is the
only condition. Thus, the meaning of the inference is (1) if
the condition is fulfilled, the consequent must be fulfilled;
(2) if the consequent is not fulfilled, the condition could not
have been fulfilled. The valid forms of reasoning from an if-
then statement, therefore, are:

CASE 5	CASE 6
If *A*, then *B;*	If *A*, then *B;*
and *A;*	and not-*B;*
therefore, *B.*	therefore, not-*A.*

Case 5 expresses logically the assurance that, given a true
causal relation, if the cause occurs, the effect must follow.
Case 6 expresses logically the point that, if the effect does not
occur, its cause could not have been enacted. This second
form indicates, as we suggested earlier, that there is an exact
and certain logical justification for the elimination of false hypotheses. If the supposed cause is enacted and the effect does

not occur, what had been conceived as a cause is not properly the cause. Or, if the deduced and predicted consequences of a hypothesis are controverted by the facts, the hypothesis must be rejected as false.

To argue from the hypothetical inference in the following ways is, however, logically incorrect:

CASE 7	CASE 8
If A, then B;	If A, then B;
and not-A;	and B;
therefore, not-B.	therefore, A.

Case 7 is not correct, for just because one condition for B, namely A, is not enacted, it does not follow that the occurrence of B could not have been brought about by another condition, say, D. Case 8 is incorrect, for the appearance of the effect B does not mean that A, one of the conditions, had to occur; another condition, D, could have been operative to produce B. Nevertheless, Case 8, as we said earlier, is the logical form for expressing the procedure for verification among the factual sciences. Since the inference from B to A is not logically necessary, the most that can be achieved in the attempt to verify a hypothesis is to set up a probability for its truth or adequacy. It cannot be put beyond the reach of doubt or revision. This is one of the reasons for the scientific enterprise's being a continuous one. As a scientific knower, man never finally arrives at a destination — he is always on the road.

The contentions we have advanced suggest that there is no distinctively empirical, or inductive, logic. The principles of inference employed in the factual sciences are exactly those studied in what is commonly called deductive logic. What is generally termed inductive logic is simply an attempt to make the principles of valid inference applicable to the scientist's attempts to construct knowledge of the phenomenal world. The rational structures and conceptual forms in which the scientist expresses his experience and his manipulative procedures are those of formal logic. Formal logic and mathematics are the languages of the factual, or empirical, sciences. Later we shall discuss the technique of problem-solving (scientific method is simply a method of solving problems). We can then show that the steps of the problem-solving process are also express-ible in the categories of deductive logic. Scientific method, or inductive logic, is an attempt to apply the categories and rules of deduction to the world of sensory experience.

In the previous chapters, we treated the nature and pro-cedures of the factual sciences with only a brief allusion or two to mathematics. Anyone who has been exposed to these sciences or to engineering practices knows that mathematical deduction plays an indispensable part in modern scientific work. To illustrate, we use an example similar to the one about the disintegration of radium. When we assert the inference, if uranium disintegrates in proportion to the mass present at any time, then in 4.6 billion years half its mass will have dis-appeared, we summarize a set of rather precise mathematical deductions. First, we turn the English expression "uranium decays in proportion to the mass present" into mathematical symbols. Disintegration of mass (M) is decay over a period of time; it is symbolized by $-dM/dt$. Hence,

$$- dM/dt = 4.8 \times 10^{-18}M,$$

where the number 4.8×10^{-18} expresses the rate of emission of atomic particles from a gram of uranium, M represents the mass of uranium, and t represents time. On this formula, we then perform a set of operations, which are a sequence of steps in deductive mathematical thought.

$$dM/M = - 4.8 \times 10^{-18}dt$$
$$\log (M/M_o) = - 4.8 \times 10^{-18}t$$
$$M = M_oe^{-4.8 \times 10^{-18}t}$$

M_o is the number of atoms of uranium at the beginning of the process. Since we want the time when half the mass of ura-nium has disintegrated, that is, when $M = M_o /2$, we write,

$$M_o/2 = M_o e^{-4.8 \times 10^{-18} t}$$
$$\tfrac{1}{2} = e^{-4.8 \times 10^{-18} t}$$
$$\log \tfrac{1}{2} = -4.8 \times 10^{-18} t$$
$$t = 10^{18} \log 2/4.8$$
$$= 1.4 \times 10^{17} \text{ seconds} = 4.6 \text{ billion years.}$$

The deductions are a set of precise logical steps from the formulation of the hypothesis in symbols to the final conclusion.

Such mathematical and logical deductions are in general closely connected with observation, manipulation, generalization, and prediction in the factual sciences. Mathematics is the language of the factual sciences. As Galileo once said, "Without mathematics I am blind." Modern science continues to bear out the ancient insight of Pythagoras that "all things are numbers," that is, the key to the understanding and description of nature is mathematics.

For another example of the methods of the formal sciences, we turn to some deductions connected with the special theory of relativity. They are of interest as a striking example of the use of deductive argument in the development of the factual sciences. Moreover, by introducing them here, we can fortify our earlier criticism of the objectivity of space and time.

First, we must indicate that the Galilei-Newtonian mechanics had its way of dealing with relative motion, one with which we are all familiar to some extent. Consider a point, O, on the bank of a river. The current runs from right to left at a rate of 4 miles per hour.

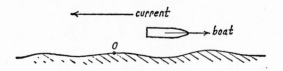

A boat travels upstream at 7 miles per hour. The boat's velocity relative to the riverbank is

$$v = v_{\text{boat}} - v_{\text{stream}} = 7 - 4 = 3 \text{ miles per hour.}$$

If we want to compute how far upstream the boat moves in 2 hours, we can use the formula, $x_2 = x_1 - vt$, where x_1 is the distance the boat would move if the water were at rest with respect to the bank and vt is the distance "lost" on account of the movement of the stream. Thus,

$$x_2 = 14 - 4(2) = 6 \text{ miles.}$$

Furthermore, it makes no difference in the analysis of the problem whether the times and distances are measured by an observer on the riverbank or one in the boat. In more general form, the Galilei-Newtonian transformations for the case of uniform velocity in a straight line are

$$\begin{cases} x_2 = x_1 - vt \\ y_2 = y_1 \end{cases}$$

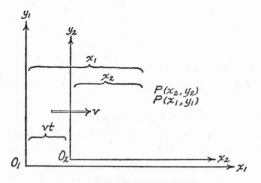

The reference framework O_2 travels at a velocity v with respect to reference framework O_1. The point P is reckoned as at a distance x_2 from O_2 and at a distance x_1 from O_1. The co-ordinates y_2 and y_1 are the same, since we are considering motion only in the x-direction. Time is the same in both systems, that is, $t_2 = t_1$. Consequently, the simple time factor t appears in the transformations.

Now let us consider the case of the propagation of light from a source O_1 to a point P.

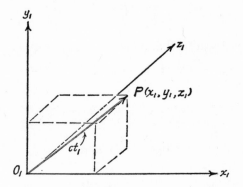

The speed of light is c ($= 300,000$ kilometers per second). We must also take account of the fact that it has been established that the velocity of light is not affected by the motion of its source. The formula expressing the transmission of a light wave from O_1 to P is:

$$x_1^2 + y_1^2 + z_1^2 = c^2 t_1^2$$

Now consider an observer in another frame of reference, O_2, moving relative to the system O_1 with a velocity v. Since the speed of the source does not affect the velocity of the propagation of light waves, the formula for the transmission of the wave in this system is:

$$x_2^2 + y_2^2 + z_2^2 = c^2 t_2^2$$

Inasmuch as the law of propagation is invariant with respect to the reference frameworks, it is necessary that the following identity obtain.

$$x_1^2 + y_1^2 + z_1^2 - c^2 t_1^2 \equiv x_2^2 + y_2^2 + z_2^2 - c^2 t_2^2 \qquad \text{(I)}$$

The Galilei-Newtonian transformations should satisfy this identity. For three-space, those transformations are

$$\begin{cases} x_2 = x_1 - vt_1 \\ y_2 = y_1 \\ z_2 = z_1 \\ t_2 = t_1. \end{cases} \qquad (II)$$

Substituting them in the identity (I), we get

$$x_1{}^2 + y_1{}^2 + z_1{}^2 - c^2t_1{}^2 \equiv (x_1 - vt_1)^2 + y_1{}^2 + z_1{}^2 - c^2t_1{}^2,$$

or

$$x_1{}^2 + y_1{}^2 + z_1{}^2 - c^2t_1{}^2 \equiv x_1{}^2 + y_1{}^2 + z_1{}^2 - c^2t_1{}^2 + v^2t_1{}^2 - 2vx_1t_1.$$

This requires that

$$v^2t_1{}^2 - 2vx_1t_1 \equiv 0.$$

That is,

$$v = 0.$$

But the condition $v = 0$ says that the system O_2 is at rest with respect to system O_1, whereas we originally assumed it to be in motion. *Reductio ad absurdum.* The Galilei-Newtonian transformations do not satisfy the identity (I). Consequently, the assumptions expressed in those transformations that space and time are independent and that time is the same in both systems must be called into question. What formulas do properly relate the two systems? The Lorentz-Einstein transformations do so. They are

$$\begin{aligned} x_2 &= (x_1 - vt_1)/\sqrt{1 - v^2/c^2} \\ t_2 &= (t_1 - vx_1/c^2)/\sqrt{1 - v^2/c^2} \\ y_2 &= y_1 \\ z_2 &= z_1. \end{aligned} \qquad (III)$$

The reader may easily satisfy himself on this score by making the appropriate substitutions. Notice that in the transformations t_2 is not in general equal to t_1. Observe also that the formula for x_2 involves t_1 and the formula for t_2 involves x_1. That is, space and time are interdependent, not independent. Time and distances measurements in O_2 of things or events in O_1 are not the same as those made by an observer in the latter system.

We can now summarize certain results that can be derived from the Lorentz-Einstein transformations (III). Consider an observer in world$_1$ (frame of reference for measurement, O_1) and another observer in world$_2$ (frame of reference for measurement, O_2), moving at velocity v with respect to world$_1$. The observer in world$_1$ notes that two events at different positions in his world are simultaneous.

For the observer in world$_2$, which travels at a high velocity with respect to world$_1$, these events are not simultaneous. As a matter of fact, in general an interval of time, T_1, in world$_1$ is measured in world$_2$ as

$$T_2 = kT_1, \text{ where } k = 1/\sqrt{1 - v^2/c^2}.$$

That is, T_2 is greater than T_1.

A set of deductions for distances measured from world$_2$ will show that

$$L_2 = \frac{1}{k} L_1.$$

That is, the observer in world$_2$ measures distances in world$_1$ as shorter than does the observer in world$_1$. Again, where v is small compared to c, L_2 is the same as L_1 for all practical purposes.

We spoke of world$_2$ as moving with respect to world$_1$. It makes no difference if we had referred to world$_1$ as moving with respect to world$_2$. Mechanically speaking, it is impossible to distinguish between the two situations. Consequently, it is clear that the concepts of the absoluteness and independence of space and time must be abandoned. As a final comment, let us say that, in cases of relative motion where v is very small compared to c, the Lorentz-Einstein transformations reduce to the Galilei-Newtonian ones. One merely needs to set $v = 0$ in the Lorentz-Einstein transformations to demonstrate this. The classical mechanics of Newton is but a special case of a more general theory of motion in a space-time continuum.

The argument pursued in developing the special theory of relativity is a striking illustration of the use of mathematical-logical techniques in dealing with a scientific problem that was posed by three main facts: (1) the finite velocity of light; (2) the velocity of light is independent of the motion of its source; and (3) the reciprocity of states of rest and of uniform rectilinear motion. A simple set of deductions results in dramatic changes in our whole scientific world view.

Modern mathematics, which has undergone very rapid development since the invention of co-ordinate geometry by Descartes (1596–1650), is an extension of logic. It is a logical discipline in which the basic categories are those of number, class membership, class inclusion, figure, continuity, and so on. One of the chief factors in the amazing growth of modern science after the sixteenth century was precisely the development of a logical language that could express quantitative relationships exactly. The invention of analytical geometry and differential calculus (Leibnitz and Newton), to mention two key disciplines, gave scientists new languages for dealing with the quantitative structure of nature, which the traditional logic of Aristotle could not effectively handle. The new language of mathematics helped to cut science loose from philosophy and theology, in which qualitative and teleological explanations, fortified by Aristotelian logic, reigned supreme. The change in languages to which we refer was comparable to the development of a precise and powerful dialect within a mother tongue. The dialect of mathematics has its root categories in formal logic. Moreover, the mother discipline of logic has itself suffered significant changes as it matured. Some of those who contributed to the development of modern symbolic logic and to the logical foundations of modern mathematics were Leibnitz, George Boole, Georg Cantor, Gottlob Frege, Augustus De Morgan, Richard Dedekind, Giuseppe Peano, A. N. Whitehead, and Bertrand Russell. The basic laws of inference and the fundamental concepts in algebra, geometry, analytical geometry, calculus, and higher disciplines are precisely those of formal or symbolic logic.

There are, then, two fundamental criteria for the evaluation of scientific propositions and arguments: truth and validity. The question of truth is the question as to whether or not the relationships among ideas asserted in propositions correspond to the relationships among facts in the phenomenal world. The question of validity is the question as to whether or not propositions are related to one another in argument in a logically consistent way, that is, without contradiction. Among other criteria, the conditions of truth and validity must be met by any structure of scientific thought.

Chapter VII

Can the Scientist Come
to Grips with God?

A scientist is rightly somewhat suspicious and hesitant to speak when men mention the problem of God. To observe, measure, and experiment with rats, dogs, and men, which are real, concrete objects, seem to be reasonable tasks to him. But one cannot see, measure, and pry into God. The science of psychology can come to terms with the man who sees a green dragon, but not with the green dragon itself. The term "God" does not signify a thing that can be publicly observed, measured, and manipulated. Therefore, it designates something with which a scientist apparently cannot deal.

There are two chief methods of inquiry used in the sciences: mathematical inquiry and empirical inquiry. From beginning to end, pure mathematics does business in terms of abstract formulations, such as number, continuity, and equality. The nature of mathematical inquiry is clearly exhibited in Euclid's geometry. One begins with definitions and postulates, which are either stipulated or assumed. He then proceeds by deducing the meanings implicitly contained in these primitive ideas and assertions. While a particular result, "The sum of the interior angles of a triangle is 180 degrees," is more specific than the typical postulate, "The whole is equal to the sum of its parts," it is no less an abstract formulation. In empirical inquiry, on the other hand, one starts with concrete facts of experience. By careful observation and prudent generalization, he arrives at results that are abstract formulations, such as

$T = k/P$ or $S = kt^2$. The laws arrived at in this way are nowhere to be found in perceptual experience. They are imposed upon or ascribed to the concrete items of first-person experience from which inquiry began. They can be termed logical constructions. Scientific knowledge, mathematical or empirical, is a matrix of abstractions. It is a rationalization of first-person experience.

In great measure, the factual sciences still employ what may be called a representative theory of knowledge. This theory asserts that there are objects "out there" beyond the perceiving subject. The structures and relations among these objects are mediated to the knower by percepts, or even perhaps by concepts. John Locke distinguished between primary and secondary ideas. The former were extension, solidity, number, figure, and motion. In Locke's opinion, they correctly represented the structures and relations among the objects "out there." The secondary ideas — for example, tastes, sounds, colors — expressed the subject's reaction to external objects but directly communicated to us nothing about those objects themselves. George Berkeley demonstrated that even the so-called primary ideas are relative to the perceiving subject. We are thus driven to the conclusion that all our knowledge is peculiarly our own. Human knowledge, common sense or scientific, is a typically human interpretation of the unknown things "out there." It follows that scientific facts, the foundations upon which the whole superstructure of scientific knowledge is built, are distinctively human responses to stimuli whose actual natures and functionings, independent of the perceiver, are unknown.

It is fortunate, however, that our percepts exhibit a degree of reliability. Furthermore, the quantitative measures we assign to them are reliable. This is what makes scientific inquiry useful. We are able to build bridges and radar networks because we "see" things in approximately the same way day after day. But, it must be remembered that the property of reliability does not tell us anything about objects in themselves but only something about the manner in which we perceive them.

What we refer to by the terms "cause" and "effect" does not provide an escape from the relativity of our knowledge. Those terms simply refer to the regular conjunction in consciousness of several events. As far as our knowledge goes, they do not denote any necessary connections, hidden efficient forces or powers, or metaphysical entities. Event *A* occurs next to event *B* once, twice, three times, . . . , a hundred times, or a thousand times. On the basis of this regularity only, we begin to speak of *A* being the cause of *B*. Even if we are able to express their conjunction or functional relationship in mathematical formulas, nothing is communicated about the objects in themselves. We are simply describing with great accuracy things and their relations as they appear to us.

Consequently, scientific knowledge has no metaphysical status. It is a knowledge of things as they appear to a human creature, with its peculiar facilities for perception, formulation (abstraction), and reaction. Science provides us with a highly detailed and very useful blueprint of the content of consciousness. The images, percepts, and concepts with which man deals are symbols for external objects, whose real structures, relations, and operations remain unknown. They may be very useful symbols, but they are still only symbols. *What* is symbolized remains unknown. Man and reality are like two physically separated lovers, who exchange endearing notes but can never look upon each other or embrace. The words in the notes are a poor compensation for the direct view of beauty and the ecstasy of embrace. What alternative, if any, is open to us if we abandon a representative theory of knowledge does not fall within the scope of this discussion.

It is clear, then, that the scientist must rule out of his inquiries the attempt to determine the (metaphysical) truth of the claim by men of mystical temperament that they personally know God. Similarly, the rules of scientific procedure require a rejection of the " divine " credentials of an authoritative literature or institution. If the term " God " is understood to mean a supernatural being, evidenced by personal experience or by an inspired book or organization, then God is the concern of someone other than the scientist.

There are, however, at least two senses in which the term " God " designates something with which the scientist can come to grips. When the term refers to an idea of very general order, bearing logical relations to other human ideas, subject to analysis or argument, and likely to influence human conduct, the scientist is as much interested in this idea as in any other. And when the word " God " stands, as it sometimes does, for a group of moral ideals (for example, benevolence, justice, prudence) or for a set of guides for conduct, again the scientist can come to terms with God. As idea or ideal, God represents a subject matter with which a man of science can deal. Our interest at this point is in the concept of God, not in faith or a sense of the reality of God. Science cannot legislate concerning the latter. The concept of God has a logical status and function. The examination of it is, therefore, relevant to the development of the underlying logics in science and religion.

The Christian tradition insists that there is more to God than the idea or the moral ideal. It is chiefly concerned with the metaphysical status of the concept of God or of other religious ideas. Its position is logically expressible in the inference: if the concept of God is true, then it is useful. The two valid forms of argument from this inference are: (I) true, therefore useful; (II) not useful, therefore not true. Since the scientist is not equipped to determine metaphysical truth, he must completely dismiss argument I. As for argument II, we can say that it represents an insistence that theological assertions that are irrelevant to human conduct (useless) be rejected. Obviously, the tradition has not always been thoroughgoing in its application of the point of this argument. It requires a pragmatic test of theological doctrines. Do they or can they make any difference in the guidance of human conduct? If not, they cannot be true. This constitutes an admirable device for stripping away from the structure of Christian thought irrelevant items, vague speculations, and useless superstitions. It is perhaps understandable that each man is persuaded that what can be cut out of the system are the beliefs of those who differ from him.

If one proceeds exclusively on the basis of argument I, useless speculative additions are likely to be made to the structure of Christian thought without limit. If the tradition were seriously to operate on the basis of argument II, it might produce a modest and useful set of ideas and ideals in which the man of science could have some confidence and in which he could invest himself. To conduct theological inquiries solely on the basis of argument II is, however, at best a negative procedure. With it one can trim away useless accretions, but he cannot add a fund of warranted assertions to the system of Christian thought.

Recalling the original inference, we emphasize that it is invalid to argue from it that because a belief is useful it is therefore true. Nevertheless, it is important to notice that the verification or corroboration of scientific hypotheses is established in this way. Hypothesis X has certain implications, A, B, and C. If X, then A, B, and C. Then A, B, and C are found to occur. The repeated occurrence of the deduced consequences of a hypothesis gives rise to a probability factor in favor of the hypothesis. At least the scientist's confidence in the hypothesis is increased, and he continues to use it. It seems reasonable to permit a religious person to be as illogical as a scientist. By analogy, we may say that in religious matters a critical use of the criterion of usefulness can set up a presumption for the truth of the concept or hypothesis of God. The usefulness of religious ideas is an indirect method of warranting the assertion of God. Religious ideas justified in this way must, of course, be held as hypotheses, not certain truths. They will be accompanied by a healthy skepticism, as are hypotheses in science. This should not strike us as a curiosity. Perhaps a mark of faith is to allow God to settle some issues and not to presume to settle them all for one's self.

Religious ideas and ideals can be justifiably held and they can be useful and edifying, provided they are considered as tentative and recognized as being subject to change with further experience. We can sum the matter up, then, by saying that (1) it is possible that a presumption for the "truth" of the idea of God may be set up by a properly devised "indirect verification," and (2) the assertion of propositions about God must be interpreted as proposals of hypotheses.

The usefulness of the idea of God can constitute a justification for the assertion of God. But another question immediately appears. Useful for what? In order to answer this question in conformity with the interests of a scientist, we may say, useful for making the human being physically and mentally healthy. A healthy organism will ordinarily be a happy one. Happiness is the emotional tone of the life of an organism that is operating smoothly, healthily, and unfrustrated by serious obstacles to the achievement of its goals.

The happy and healthy life is not, however, necessarily one where there is a complete absence of despair, misery, conflict, and senses of shame and guilt. Solving problems is integral to the process of living. The healthy must confront problems, and they are therefore beset by the perplexity, despair, and inner turmoil that accompany their appearance. Everyone meets problems as long as he lives, whether he is healthy or ill. The only question is whether or not a man is strong enough to come through periods of despair and anxiety with his integrity and health unimpaired. The measure of a strong personality is not how little misery it suffers, but how much misery it can overcome. An idea of God can be considered useful if it can be successfully employed to unify and fortify a person so that he can ably meet and solve his problems and emerge in a healthy state, rather than be seriously damaged in body and mind by his problems and the symptoms that attend them. On the other hand, religious ideas and techniques that overwhelm people with a sense of shame and guilt or directly enhance anxiety and despair are destructive of personality and must be rejected.

What cardinal virtues should be fostered under the idea of God in order to contribute to physical and mental health? By what criteria can we judge whether or not an idea of God is useful? We propose that a religious idea be tentatively accepted or rejected on the basis of whether or not it fosters *integrity, compassion,* and *humility.* These virtues are symptoms of and are conducive to mental and physical health. If any religious idea or system fails to foster them, it is summarily to be rejected, regardless of other evidence brought forward on its behalf.

Ordinarily a man of integrity is thought of as an honest man, one who does not lie. But integrity means something more profound and more directly related to health than honesty. A life of integrity is an *integral* life, that is, it is a life characterized by soundness, unity, and a certain purposiveness. The integral personality is the polar opposite of the personality that betrays divisiveness, indecision, and a lack of reflective foresight and resolution. Integrity means healthy unity in body and mind. The man of integrity has to some degree organized and related his various desires and propensities to action under the control of a single concept, goal, or loyalty. The idea of God, modestly and reasonably framed, can serve as the high loyalty under which a man's life is rendered integral. It would scarcely be reasonable to insist, however, that any particular religious tradition has a monopoly on the God-idea which is useful for fostering integrity in personality. A man is not truly humane and healthy unless he has integrity, and this seems to require a sovereign loyalty at work unifying the sinews of personality.

The second criterion is compassion. Unfortunately, this term has acquired sentimentalistic connotations. It is, however, considerably more satisfactory than love or pity. For our purposes, it is best to think of compassion as empathy, a facility to feel one's self to be in another's situation and to guide one's conduct in accord with that intuitive appreciation of the other person and his problems. The first criterion is intended to specify the necessity of each man's being a strong, organized, distinctive personality. This second criterion simply emphasizes that no man can become healthy and humane in isolation. Mental and physical health require sympathetic relations with other persons. We should also take note of Nietzsche's admonition at this point. He says that pity (*Mitleid*) is not itself a virtue, but *being able to stand* that you have compassion upon others is a real virtue.[3] For if empathy goes to an extreme, it results in a revulsive sentimentality or in an abnormal identification with another person. To be healthy and humane requires affective relations with other persons and their problems, while retaining one's own identity, integrity, and self-respect. These first two criteria are like two magnetic poles, in tension between which the person must live if he is to live sanely and healthily. Only the man of a strong character can really have compassion on others and out of that compassion render real service to their needs. A man who is physically and mentally unstable can only pity others (and himself), and he is incapacitated for ministering to them. An idea of God may be considered to be justified to the extent that it fosters this creative rapport between persons called compassion.

The scribes and Pharisees brought to Jesus a woman taken in adultery, saying to him, "Teacher, the law commands us that such a sinner be stoned; what do you say?" But Jesus stooped down and with his finger wrote on the ground, as though he did not hear them. When they pressed for an answer, he said, "Let the man among you who is without sin cast the first stone." And again he stooped down and scribbled in the dust. Being convicted in their own consciences, the accusers went away. When Jesus arose, he said to her, "Woman, where are those who accuse you?" The insensitive and complacent accusers of the woman saw only that she had offended against the law. They spat out vindictive and caustic words of condemnation. "She should be stoned! What do you say?" This is the noisy, inhumane, and vicious attitude of men who criticize others while overlooking their own offenses. Jesus stooped down and scribbled in the dust, as if the hammering of their words against his ears spelled out no meaning. Silence is frequently the most severe rebuke we can give to an insensitive adversary in whom words substitute for thought and insight. Jesus had compassion upon the woman, but only severe silence for her judges. Authentic religion — the spirit of integrity and compassion — is displayed here in opposition to the severity and legalism of the customary ethical standards of society and the authoritarian spirit of a church and its agents. A sane and sincere religion requires that we, like Jesus, have the courage and compassion to reckon the wayward, the sick, and the infirm, the outcast and the alien, as our equals in the sight of God. A faith that lacks such universal sensitivity and compassion is neither very humane nor very religious. In answer to this demand, men do not look for words but for deeds. Frequently there is a refreshing frankness among the writers in the Bible, as when one wrote, " If a man says he loves God and hates his brother, he is a liar; for how can he love God, whom he does not see, when he cannot love his brother, whom he does see? " The passage in the Gospel of John that relates the story of the woman taken in adultery (ch. 8:1-11) is in question from a critical point of view. It is, however, a penetrating analysis of the attitude of a truly religious person.

The third criterion is humility. To be humble is not to be humiliated. The humiliated man is one who is weak, beaten down by the fortunes of life, overwhelmed with problems that leave him in despair and without hope. He is physically and mentally ill. He lacks the psychological or spiritual resources to deal effectively with his problems and to conquer despair and anxiety. On the other hand, the humble man is one who has integrity, health, and strength, but who recognizes all the while that he is a man and not a god. He feels competent to deal with life's problems, but, in a knowledge of his strength, he refrains from arrogance and conceit. The strong man, because he is strong, is able to be humble. The weak man is a humiliated person who tries to compensate for his weakness by putting up a front of arrogance, aggressiveness, and pretentiousness. Humility in a person is a symptom of that person's recognition of his finitude. The idea of God is justifiable in so far as it can generate strong personalities who cannot be humiliated by life's problems but who, through their strength as well as their recognition of their finitude, are humble.

If a man does not have integrity, compassion, and humility, he is neither quite the humane creature he might be nor is he the Christian character he may pretend to be by his confessions, rituals, and conventional respectability. The concept of God, understood as the antecedent of the inference we mentioned earlier, is a hypothesis for religious living. It is a hypothesis whose content is the idea that all the world can be understood under one universal category. As a hypothesis, it is used for guidance in solving problems, just as in science hypotheses are used for such guidance. By it, that sovereign loyalty can be introduced into the human person which results in the integrity, sensitivity, and humility constituting authentic humanity.

If the concept of God is true, then it is useful. Useful for what? Useful for fostering healthy persons, that is, persons characterized by integrity, compassion, and humility. These are distinctively humane and healthy marks of personality. The idea of God is justified on the condition that it is useful in producing this type of person. Otherwise, it is not warranted. A scientist can come to grips with God on some such terms as these. Perhaps these are exactly the terms which are really important, for they involve the questions of respect for personality and of humane stature among men. At this crucial point, the rational interests of science and the humane interests of religion coincide.

Chapter VIII

Solving Problems and Thinking God

We have referred to the idea of God as a hypothesis that is used for solving problems that appear in the process of living. We also stated some terms under which a theological hypothesis can be considered warranted and, therefore, be continued in use. Let us now examine more carefully the problem-solving process, for it seems that both scientific inquiry and religious inquiry are methods of solving problems.

Everyone knows what a problem is. More accurately, everyone knows *when* he is confronted by a problem. To be in a problem situation is to be anxious, perplexed, or emotionally and physically disturbed. While everyone knows when he is anxious and distressed, hardly anyone can adequately express in words what a problem or problem situation is. The best that we can do is to allude to the nature of a problem situation, just as one must allude to other intimate and immediate experiences, such as love, pleasure, pain, and joy.

Let us, therefore, suggest rather than define the nature of a problem situation. It is one in which the normal equilibria of the human person are disturbed. It is a state of physical, emotional, or intellectual instability. When our normal habits of thought fail in a critical situation or when our ordinary habits of overt behavior are obstructed, we become tense, uneasy, or anxious. These disturbances of our natural equilibria exhibit themselves in the symptoms of nausea, distress, despair, perplexity, or suicidal behavior. Body, mind, and affections are simply different aspects of the functional whole of personality. Thus, there is probably no purely intellectual disturbance, unaccompanied by dissonances in bodily functioning and in the flow of affections; there is no physical disturbance without its repercussions at the levels of feeling and thinking. But in some problem situations the intellectual element is dominant, as when the perplexity arises from considering the possibility of trisecting an angle by straightedge and compass. In others, the unrest is primarily affective; and in yet others, the symptoms indicate that the root of the problem is in a physiological disturbance, resulting, for example, from the immodest consumption of alcoholic beverages or from a blow to the stomach. In problem situations generally, our normal habits of thought and behavior are interrupted, and our attempts to reach an intended or desired goal are thwarted. This interruption of the organism's ordinary functions disturbs its equilibria, causing perplexity, anxiety, physical or emotional revulsion, or senseless utterances and gestures.

Taking a slightly different point of view, we can say that a problem situation arises when something novel enters the intellectual, emotional, or physical environment of the organism. The novel item – a peculiar idea, a significant question, an insult, an unseemly sight, an unusual animal, an impeding object, or a goldfish in mid-throat – constitutes a unique, puzzling spot in the comfortable and orderly environment in which the organism had been living with relative ease. It blocks the habitual lines of thought and conduct and causes hesitation, perplexity, or anxiety. It demands an adjustment of habits. When the problem is of some magnitude, the anxiety and distress of the organism are acute and its actions are disjointed and awry. If it is not solved and the anxiety relieved or overcome, the organism may be permanently impaired. To be sure, some problems are of slight significance – as when the habit of brushing one's teeth is stalled by an empty toothpaste tube – and they can be overlooked or handled by substituting other habits. We are chiefly concerned with problems of some magnitude in science and religion. The failure to solve certain problems in science and religion can result in misery and catastrophe for many men and nations. The failure to solve crucial religious problems can produce moral corruption, despair, and insanity among men.

How are problems solved by the scientist or, for that matter, by any person who tries to deal with them intelligently? There is a logical structure to the rational problem-solving process. Once a problem occurs, four steps are taken that, if successful, bring the problem to solution.

First, there must be some sort of definition of what the problem is. Sitting at leisure some evening in his living room, a man may suddenly be invaded by the feeling that something is wrong or different in his environment. He feels uneasy and senses that the normal context of his living room world has been disturbed. By focusing attention here and there, he quickly canvasses his environment and discovers that the radio which had been supplying music is now silent. Perhaps he verbalizes his problem by a simple question such as, "What happened to the radio?" This step in definition or diagnosis may be taken so quickly in many problem situations that we are not ordinarily aware of its occurrence. It is necessary, however, for the problem solver to probe beneath the symptoms of a problem situation (perplexity, anxiety, etc.) and to define in some measure what it is that causes his uneasiness or distress. Definition, analysis, or verbalization must occur before any other controlled step toward the solution of the problem can be taken. Of course, not all problems have a short and simple first stage. In many scientific and engineering problems, much time and energy will be invested in analyzing and defining precisely the nature of the problem situation before any further headway is made. Some problems remain in the stage of definition for a period of years or generations.

Once a definition of the problem is at hand, the second step can be taken. When the mind entertains a clear conception of what the problem is, certain suggestions for its solution occur. The nature, number, and relevance of these suggestions undoubtedly depend upon the past experience, knowledge, and creative imagination of the person confronting the problem. However that may be, one does not deliberately produce or manufacture the suggestions. They are " given " in consciousness. They appear there unheralded. A person's apprehension of them is, properly speaking, an intuitive experience. The logical form for expressing this stage of the problem-solving process is an alternative proposition: either A, or B, or C, or D. In the example introduced above, when the man who is suddently deprived of his music recognizes what the problem is, he has certain suggestions occur to him. " Either the baby pulled the power cord from the electrical outlet, or my wife shut the radio off while I was engrossed in my reading, or a radio tube failed, or the electrical supply to the house has gone off." The subject will not lack for suggestions in a simple situation such as this. In more complex problem situations, there may be a dearth of suggestions. In such a case, one simply prowls around in the context until one or another suggestion appears.

After the occurrence of some suggestions, a third step can be taken. The consequences of the suggestions are inferred. The logical form for this stage of the process is given by the hypothetical inference: if A, then X. Thus, our subject with the mute radio thinks, " If the baby pulled the cord from the outlet, then I should be able to see the disconnected power cord when I step over to the radio; if my wife turned the radio off, then I can restore the music by turning the switch on again; if one of the tubes is bad, then I can discover whether this is so by looking to see if the filaments are heated; if the house's electrical supply is interrupted, then I can discover whether this is the case by trying to switch on the ceiling lamp." These steps in the problem-solving process are mental inferences. They attempt to draw out the detailed meanings of the suggestions, so that these suggestions can be put to tests to determine their correctness or adequacy. In their most exact and rigorous form, they are made in accord with valid logical (or mathematical) patterns of argument. Scientific and technological problems generally demand at this step a chain of mathematical deductions. Recalling the example used earlier concerning the disintegration of uranium, the steps traversed there were an illustration of the inferential part of a rational problem-solving process.

Finally, when the consequences of the suggestions are deduced or inferred, they are put to the test. This may be considered verification. The man who is concerned about his malfunctioning radio proceeds, perhaps, in this way. Stepping over to the radio, he sees that the power cord is not disconnected and concludes that the suggestion that the baby disconnected it is wrong. He calls a question to his wife; she answers that she did turn it off because she thought he was not listening to it. Stepping to the radio, he turns the switch on again and in a few seconds the music is restored to his environment. His problem is solved. The logical form of this last step is specified by the meaning of the hypothetical proposition: if A, then X; and not-X; therefore, not-A. This form of argument is used to reject suggestions or hypotheses whose deduced consequences do not occur. It secures a definitive rejection of faulty or improper suggestions. Where a suggestion is correct or proper, the invalid form of argument characteristic of the process of verification is used to warrant it. If B, then Y; and Y; therefore, B. We will not repeat here the comments made earlier on this mode of inference.

These are the temporally successive steps used in the rational problem-solving process, whether the problems are those of everyday life, of ethical options, or of the scientific laboratory. They can be summarized schematically in this way:

(1) The problem is Q.
(2) Suggestions for solution: either A, or B, or C.

(3) Deduction of consequences: if *A*, then *X*;
         if *B*, then *Y*;
         if *C*, then *Z*.

(4) Verification: not-*X*; therefore, not-*A*;
      not-*Y*; therefore, not-*B*;
      Z, therefore, (probably) *C*.

And enact *C* for (possible) final solution to *Q*.

According to our earlier discussion, scientific method is a procedure for solving certain types of human problems. The outline we have given suggests that the rational problem-solving process is expressible in the categories of logic. In elementary fashion, we have thus indicated that there is no unique inductive logic, but that the formal structure of scientific method is that of deductive logic.

Problems fall roughly into two groups: theoretical ones and practical ones. Practical problems require overt action of some kind to bring them to solution. That is, they require the fourth step, verification. Problems in the domains of the factual sciences are of this type. The problem of the man who is uneasy because the music had dropped out of his environment is a practical one. So also is the problem related to the question about how uranium disintegrates. On the other hand, theoretical problems are ones that are completed at the end of the third step and require no verification. They are problems of thought. They occur frequently in mathematics, formal logic, philosophy, and theology. There is no possibility of verifying solutions to theoretical problems by checking them against the facts, for such problems do not refer to factual data in the first place. They are concerned with properly relating abstract ideas to one another. The demonstrations of the propositions in Euclidean geometry are good, simple examples of solutions for theoretical problems.

What does it mean, then, to solve a problem? It means to *rationalize* the novel. Few problem situations are so threatening or devastating as to result in death if they go unsolved;

but some are of such a degree of severity. Problems of great magnitude or importance must be solved if a person is to live, or at least if he is to live healthily. A person is in some measure ill — physically, emotionally, or intellectually — if his major problems go unsolved and if the anxiety or distress attending them is not dissipated. When a problem is solved, the novel has been rationalized in this sense: old habits of thought and action have been adjusted in order to permit the novel item to be assimilated into one's environment. A solution is generally constructed from the stuff of old thoughts, old feelings, and old habits of overt behavior. Some chance thought or rationally constructed hypothesis suddenly reveals similarities between the novel and the old images and concepts. Some chance gesture or some deliberately devised experiment discloses constituents in the novel similar to those in the familiar things in one's customary world. When lines of meaningful connection are built into the novel by the readjustment of old thoughts and modes of conduct, the novel begins to be rationalized, anxiety and distress begin to subside, and awry gestures begin to take on a deliberate, coherent, or consistent character. Finally, the problem is solved — and, as a result, the world has been transformed. The process of living is a continuous process of problem-solving, that is, of rationalizing the novel. To be living is, therefore, to be always engaged in transforming one's world. Science is a technique for bringing this creative work under the direction of reason.

Before we comment on problem-solving in man's religious life, we should observe that the human person who solves problems is more than a naked intellect. Personality is a functional unity of body, affections, and intelligence, no one of which is autonomous. It is the whole person who confronts and solves a problem, not just a thing of flesh and bone, not simply a disembodied intellect, and not merely a bundle of awry affections. When by a process of deduction a man solves the problem of the sum of the interior angles of a plane triangle, the physical adjustments correlated with his mental maneuvers may be incipient or below the threshold of consciousness, but they are nevertheless there. If he makes a predominantly affective adjustment from revulsion upon seeing his neighbor to a joyous attraction toward him, there are undoubtedly physical and conceptual changes taking place within him, although they may be masked by the emotional impact of the transformation. Heartbeat, reverie, metabolism, love, rational argument, joy, and twitching of the toe are all interrelated functions of the whole person who is engaged in solving problems.

What, however, is the primary force at work in the development of the person's so-called spiritual life? By " spirit" we mean those aspects of the person which display themselves in flights of imagination, philosophical inquiry, love and hate, mythmaking, pious aspiration, sentiment for moral ideals, reverie, and the other odds and ends of what is termed the intellectual and emotional life of man. The primordial force in man as person is an affective conation. Men generally act, not so much on the basis of what they think, but in accord with how they feel about persons and things. It is a man's temperament that largely determines the lines along which his thinking will proceed. He feels, wishes, hopes, and rejoices; and at an intellectual level these basic urges will be rationalized by him. That which leaves him cold, is avoided or hated by him, or is confusing or obscure to him will be rendered irrational and absurd at the level of comprehension. The reason, or intellect, is only one tool of the whole person. What a person feels to be real the intellect will rationalize. What he senses to be unreal the tool of reason will render irrational.

Man is a double-valued creature. Deep in his nature, there are rooted both creative and destructive impulses and energies. Within him, we find the core of what we deem orderly, good, pleasing, and exhilarating. But we find there also — seated just as firmly in the ground of being — the roots of what we consider to be chaotic, evil, painful, and depressing. Two gods are incarnate in man — *Zoe* (Freud's *Eros*) and *Thanatos*. Human behavior is the battlefield for the contest between these Pro-

methean powers. Their struggle is what chiefly moves man to
act in this way or that way. Man's reason is a weapon at hand
for both contestants. Thus, our earlier discussion of scientific
methods and knowledge should not be interpreted as meaning
that man as scientific knower is essentially, or even chiefly, a
rational being. The lines along which men solve their problems, including those of science, and the vectors along which
scientific knowledge is acquired are not dictated solely by
reason. They are fixed by the hidden gods within. Scientific
tools in the hands of men continuously remake the world. Reason alone does not guide those hands. Consequently, some
other, moral ministry, different from the resources and ministrations of science, must give a measure of guidance and direction to those hands by bringing the inner gods under control.
This is one of the points at which religion supplements science
in order to effect salvation in the human person.

To try to deal with God at the level of conceptualization is
not really to deal with God but to entertain and manipulate
an idea of deity. The idea of deity is one of the most abstract
of the family of concepts — it is of the same genre as the abstract ideas of cause, substance, energy, and the space-time
continuum. The idea of God rationalizes a person's world, expressing the vague sense he has of the fundamental unity that
underlies the flux and varieties of experience. Theological inquiries are quests at a high level of abstraction, and they handle problems of a highly intellectual and theoretical character.
Even empirical theology finds its issue in a system of abstract,
universal propositions, just as empirical science results in sets
of such propositions. Systems of theology, whether deductively
propagated or empirically constructed, are matrices of abstractions. The idea of deity constitutes the logical center of the
system and it is expected to be necessarily related to all the
details of the system.

Human problem-solving in both science and religion is simply a way of rationalizing the world. In science, the results of
the applications of various canons of inquiry are a set of ab-

stract hypotheses. These hypotheses form a kind of hierarchy as a result of the scientist's attempts to formulate fewer, more comprehensive descriptive principles. Science tries to make the world conform to the demands for logical unity, consistency, simplicity, and elegance among hypotheses. These hypotheses also formulate for the scientist how he shall go about solving problems in the future. The idea of God has the same logical status in the experience and thinking of religious persons. It is an attempt to rationalize human experience by means of a highly abstract idea. It brings coherence and consistency into the world and it is supposed to suggest how future problems of human conduct can be solved. The idea of God is a single, most universal concept, under whose conceptual simplicity the unity of the variegated world is described. Its logical function is somewhat comparable to, say, a formulation in science of an electromagnetic field theory. It is the supreme rationalization of the human spirit. One of its distinctive merits is, of course, that it invites and directs the expenditures of moral energies among men. It thus becomes relevant to the contest between the creative and destructive powers rooted in man and in nature. The idea of God moves man to cast his lot with *Zoe* rather than with *Thanatos* and to participate in the struggle to secure victory for those powers which contribute to humane existence.

Our discussion suggests, then, some relations between science and religion. Both disciplines are essentially problem-solving processes. Both result in hypotheses that express the orderliness of life and of the world as they appear to human creatures. Both use their hypotheses to control the world and to guide men in their attempts to solve problems. In both cases, inasmuch as the formulations that result from problem-solving are abstractions that outstrip the limited experience on which they are based, they must be considered as hypothetical and, therefore, subject to revision with future experience. With some justification, the scientist points out that his generalizations are always made in close connection with factual data and that they are constantly checked against those data. Generalizations in the domains of religious inquiry are not so cautious. Sometimes the religious thinker takes spectral evidence seriously. It is also clear that the scientist refuses to contend that his hypotheses have any metaphysical status, while religious persons generally maintain that the idea of God has a metaphysical referent. The idea of God has, however, the same logical status and function as the most abstract scientific formulations. Both the religious and the scientific hypothesis rationalize the world for men, and each is used to remake the world. The religious hypothesis has a moral appeal and function that relates it to the urgent and interminable contest between *Zoe* and *Thanatos* in man and in nature.

Chapter IX

Logic and Scripture

" And the Lord said, . . . 'Come, let us go down, and there confuse their language.'" At the very beginning of the Bible, the misfortunes of confused speech are memorialized in the story of the tower of Babel. God feared the power that comes to man with the use of clear and consistent speech. Words express life and energy. They are vehicles of a power sufficient to cause distress even among the gods. How great the power of man can be if his words are clear and useful! And how miserable is his situation when his words are empty names or when their meanings are obscure!

The first story of creation relates that order was brought forth from chaos when God spoke, " Let there be light." As instruments of divine speech, the prophets open their mouths to declare, " Thus says the Lord." In Amos, Jeremiah, and others, the utterance of God's words was equivalent to the initiation of divine power in the human situation. " Is not my word like fire, says the Lord, and like a hammer which breaks the rock in pieces? " (Jer. 23:29.) A psalmist records for us that God uttered his voice and the earth melted. And Joel cries out, " And the Lord roars from Zion, and utters his voice from Jerusalem, and the heavens and the earth shake." The writer of Hebrews warns that we heed " him that speaketh from heaven: whose voice then shook the earth " (ch. 12:25-26). The Bible is a commemoration of the power of words, that is, of the idea that words are pregnant with good or evil for those who utter them or hear them. It is, therefore, appropriately called the Word of God, the instrument for the communication of the life and virtues of the divine speaker. The myth of the tower of Babel expresses more than the memory of an ancient imposing edifice; its real meaning is the message concerning the critical importance of communication for human life. It is a semantic foreword to the Bible.

The Bible is an instrument of communication. The vehicles of communication are word symbols and propositions. Logic and semantics study the meanings of words and propositions. Consequently, they have something to say about Biblical communication.

Very seldom do men hear or read precisely what is said or written by another. Of course, they hear the vocal sounds and see the written symbols. Few men, however, probe effectively enough behind the symbols that they seize the meaning intended by the speaker or writer. Moreover, all are prone to read their own thoughts into words used by others. Their own sentiments and prejudices find expression in the oral or written symbols used by the speaker or writer. In such circumstances, there is really very little actual communication. Confusion and ignorance parade under the pretense of understanding. There may be a meeting of feet under a conference table, but there is no real meeting of minds. One can pick a communication situation almost at random and find an example of how the use of words blocks rather than facilitates communication. Words are vehicles of power; but they are often instruments of a power that produces misunderstanding, irritation, violence, and conceit.

The Bible must be heard. But this hearing cannot be awry responses to oral or written symbols themselves. It must be an apprehension of the *meanings* of the symbols. When Biblical communication breaks down as a result of men's failure to probe behind symbols to meanings, the Bible itself is actually destructive of real faith and healthy religious living.

In the interests of effective communication, it is important to understand that language has different functions. Some of them are: the logical function; the ceremonial function; the directive function; the expressive function; and the poetic function. Since this topic has some bearing on interpreting Biblical symbols, we describe each briefly.

1. *The Logical Function.* Language is used in its logical function when it is used to communicate information or to express argument. Ordinarily its specific form is declarative sentences which express propositions. Propositions are assertions that are subject to being true or false. " This chair has a weak leg." " Joshua and his troops conquered Jericho." " I see a red ant beside the leaf." " All mammals are sentient beings; and, whales are mammals; therefore, they are sentient." " King David reigned over Judah for seven years and over the united kingdom for thirty-three years." These sentences express propositions. The fragments of historical information in the Bible are expressed or can be expressed in propositions.

2. *The Ceremonial Function.* The ceremonial function of language is exhibited when language is used to initiate conversation or communication or to facilitate social relations. " How do you do? " " Your party was very enjoyable." " Did you hear what the Irish did to the Sooners on Saturday? " " Glad to see you; stop in again." Such sentences do not communicate information; nor do they often express sincere feelings. They are ceremonial " openers " for further conversation. They maintain a somewhat friendly atmosphere when persons have very little of real value to say to one another. The " small talk " of acquaintances is mostly of this type. Much of the liturgy of religious services or celebrations is of a ceremonial nature. We do not say that the ceremonial function of language has no value. As a matter of fact, it maintains harmonious relationships, promotes courtesy, enhances friendly feelings, avoids embarrassment, and gives people feelings of satisfaction and joy. It does not, however, communicate information. If the ceremonial function is confused with the logical one, confusion and misunderstanding result.

3. *The Directive Function.* Often language is used primarily to provoke certain types of behavior in others or to control their behavior. " Shut the window! " " Thou shalt not kill." " No man who respects the great heritage of freedom symbolized by the magnificent figure of Thomas Jefferson will fail to vote for Thomas T. Trump." " Look both ways before you cross the street." " Repent, for the kingdom of God is at hand." " Tell him that I am in the laboratory." Often political speeches and religious discourses, quite lengthy and deceptively eloquent, are simply extended discourses whose main functions are to get people to act in ways in which the speakers wish them to act.

4. *The Expressive Function.* Used in its expressive function, language is employed to give verbal form to inner feelings. Curses, songs, exclamations, and fervent editorials are good illustrations. " The damn fool! " " What an inspiring sermon! " " No freedom-loving American can tolerate the use of Quigsby's red-tainted textbook in our school." " I'll never forget you." " I saw the Lord high and lifted up." " I felt the word of God, burning as a fire in my bones." " Oh, that I had in the wilderness a lodging place of wayfaring men; that I might leave my people." The main function of this sort of speech is to give expression to one's own feelings, attitudes, emotions, prejudices, and temperament. Sometimes these utterances take the outward form of questions, declarations of fact, or argument; but it is usually clear that the speaker is not so much questioning or informing as he is giving expression to his own feelings.

5. *The Poetic Function.* The poetic function of language is closely related to the expressive function. Poetic language certainly expresses the speaker's feelings or responses. But it does not merely express; it also attempts to communicate effectively those feelings to another. It attempts to transmit not simply information but qualitative meaning. This qualitative meaning is conveyed more by the poetic form — rhythm, picturesque and musical words, metaphor, repetition, and similarity and con-

trast in sound qualities – than it is by the literal meanings of the words employed. The poet appeals, suggests, and persuades by the beauty and form of his discourse until the hearer can experience in some measure the feelings that the poet had, and can apprehend in some degree the values the poet sensed. Feeling is put into aesthetic form for communication. Poetic language communicates; but it communicates chiefly values.

Most extended speeches or writings exhibit a mixture of the several functions of language. A sermon, for example, may open and close with the ceremonial remarks, " In the name of the Father, and the Son, and the Holy Ghost," and " Amen." The introduction may exhibit mainly the logical function by using an illustration from contemporary life or by giving a description of a historical situation in Biblical times. The body of the sermon may use the logical, expressive, directive, and poetic functions. Essays, editorials, political speeches, lectures, and books generally make use of all these functions. A proper understanding of the various parts of the discourse depends upon making a right judgment as to what function is displayed at any point. It would be tragic, for example, if someone thought that Jesus' words about plucking out the offending eye and severing the offending hand were sober, authoritative uses of language in its logical and directive functions (and this has happened!). We must interpret the *parts* of a long discourse correctly. It is also imperative to make a proper judgment as to what the *over-all* function of a man's speech or writing is. A sermon may have ceremonial, expressive, and logical parts, while its over-all function is directive. If one does not perceive this, he will seriously misinterpret the speaker's meaning (by interpreting the parts aside from the context of the whole) and deceive himself. One must judge correctly the speaker's *main* purpose by discovering what over-all function his language performs.

The story of Abraham, which celebrates the father of faith, exhibits in its various parts language used logically, directively, ceremonially, and expressively. But this story has as its main function the poetic one of communicating to the reader the richness of the writer's intuition of the exhilaration, power, and significance of Abraham's faith. The story *as a whole* is not told merely for ceremonial purposes, or solely to impart so much information, or simply as an expression of the writer's feelings. Above all, the writer wanted to communicate values to the hearer or reader and also to provoke a certain kind of religious response in him. If the reader thinks that the story as a whole is a logical structure, he will, by interpreting it literally, not merely involve himself in historical absurdities but also very likely miss the real meaning that the writer intended to communicate. There is as much sense in interpreting the Abraham story literally as there is in interpreting the Paul Bunyan saga literally because one thinks that the storyteller was using language logically. The function with which language is used determines the type of interpretation that must be used to discover its real meaning. It is of utmost importance, then, to make a correct judgment about the main function(s) of the Biblical literature *as a whole*.

The ancient heroes of which the Bible speaks and also the sages who wrote the Biblical texts were a particularly unscientific lot. The Hebrews and Jews distinguished themselves in some ways, but they certainly did not do so in science and philosophy. Their temperament seemed to be adverse to critical and analytical thought. Here we come upon one important feature distinguishing Greek culture, with its Plato, Aristotle, and Democritus, from Hebrew culture, with its Amos, David, and Jeremiah. The Greeks made a name for themselves in the physical sciences, mathematics, and philosophy. The Greek mind was critical, analytical, skeptical, and capable of sustaining long, consistent lines of rational argument. The philosophical systems of Plato, Aristotle, the Pythagoreans, the Stoics, and the Epicureans, with their precise scientific and philosophical vocabularies, are dramatic symptoms of the rationalistic bent of the Greek mind. Contrast such works with those of the Bible. Hardly anywhere in the Old Testament, except in

Ecclesiastes (from the Greek period of Jewish history), does one find anything like the discourses of Plato's *Dialogues* or Aristotle's *Metaphysics*. The Hebrew mind simply was not a scientific one. While the Greeks will argue for or against the existence of a deity and write extensive, acute analyses of the attributes of a possible God, it seems never to have occurred to the Hebrew mind to argue about God. Nowhere in the Old Testament is there a systematic treatment of the nature of God. The Hebrews simply sensed the presence of God in their lives. Their writings about God are, therefore, not analytical or critical. On the contrary, they celebrate the exhilarating presence of deity in their lives.[4]

To the Hebrew mind the world was not an impersonal, mechanical object. It was not a machine, to be analyzed, dismantled, and repaired. The Hebrew proceeded on the axiom that nature was a living being, a personal entity. One does not analyze and manipulate a " personal world." He converses with it, responds to it, cultivates its friendship, and avoids its wrath. The Hebrew conversed and communed with nature, as one human person does with another. He approached the world with wonder, respect, and circumspection. He met it with his heart as much as with his mind. His perspective on nature was naïve; but there was a certain wisdom in the naïveté, to which many Greek philosophers and scientists were dense. There is a whole qualitative aspect to nature that only such an approach as the Hebrew made can properly appreciate.

The Hebrew did not argue about God. He sensed the reality of God in his life and in the realm of nature; that is, he had faith in God. His relationship to deity and nature was not that of a rational analyst. He experienced an immediate qualitative sense of the reality of God and of the power of God infusing nature. It was a cognitive experience: he knew that he was in communion with a personal power that had taken the initiative in making its presence felt. The richness and exhilaration of the experience were more than could be adequately expressed in logical propositions. The Hebrew did not deal with a conception of God but intuitively apprehended the reality of the personality of God. He was one person communicating and communing with another, higher person. The certainty of this mystical relationship far outstripped the force that any argument could exert over his mind. In the Bible we have, therefore, a record, not of the Hebrew intellect's manipulating a hypothesis of God, but of the Hebrew person's pilgrimage in and celebration of a faith in God.

What is the most natural and adequate way of expressing in language the meaning of faith? No man who has been caught up in such an experience will express it primarily in ceremonial, directive, or logical language. The verbal forms appropriate for it are those which are expressive and poetical. If we may use the analogy of the experience of love, it is clear that the lover's experience will not erupt at a verbal level mainly in ceremonial phrases, in prescriptions for behavior, or in scientific specifications of the symptoms of the experience. The experience of love is not fully comprehended in a description of a flushed face, dilation of the pupils, increased heartbeat, and vacillating gestures. The most appropriate verbal form for personal, immediate experiences such as this is poetry. Through its aesthetic forms poetry communicates more of the real richness and meaning of such experiences than any other form of expression can. Religious faith also finds its most honest and adequate display in the expressive and poetic functions of language. Consequently, we contend that the chief function of language in the Biblical literature is the poetic function. It was most appropriate for expressing the sort of experience the Hebrews had of God and of nature. Let us, therefore, admit that the Hebrews and the writers of the Biblical literature generally had more sense than is sometimes attributed to them. They were "logical" enough to know that faith had to be expressed in poetry, an alogical, symbolic form.

One example will make the point clear. We do not choose a case of the expression of the religious experience per se but one that deals with a certain aspect of nature. Both Aristotle and Amos had occasion to express themselves on the seemingly inescapable nature of causal relations. The two presentations dramatize the contrast between the Greek and Hebrew minds that we have been trying to indicate.

Aristotle says:

" Cause " means (1) that from which, as immanent material, a thing comes into being, e.g., the bronze is the cause of the statue and the silver of the saucer, and so are the classes which include these. (2) The form or pattern, i.e., the definition of the essence, and the classes which include this (e.g., the ratio 2:1 and number in general are causes of the octave), and the parts included in the definition. (3) That from which the change or the resting from change first begins; e.g., the adviser is a cause of the action, and the father a cause of the child, and in general the maker a cause of the thing made and the change-producing of the changing. (4) The end, i.e., that for the sake of which a thing is; e.g., health is the cause of walking. For " why does one walk? " we say; " that one may be healthy "; and in speaking thus we think we have given the cause. . . .

These, then, are practically all the senses in which causes are spoken of, and as they are spoken of in several senses it follows both that these are the several causes of the same thing, and in no accidental sense (e.g., both the art of sculpture and the bronze are causes of the statue not in respect of anything else but qua statue; not, however, in the same way, but the one as matter and the other as source of the movement), and that things can be causes of one another (e.g., exercise of good condition, and the latter of exercise; not, however, in the same way, but the one as end, and the other as source of movement).[5]

Now hear the herdsman of Tekoa:

Hear this word that the Lord has spoken against you, O people of Israel, against the whole family which I brought up out of the land of Egypt:

" You only have I known of all the families of the earth; therefore I will punish you for all your iniquities.

Do two walk together, unless they have made an appointment?
Does a lion roar in the forest, when he has no prey?
Does a young lion cry out from his den, if he has taken nothing?
Does a bird fall in a snare on the earth, when there is no trap for it?
Does a snare spring up from the ground, when it has taken nothing?
Is a trumpet blown in a city, and the people are not afraid?
Does evil befall a city, unless the Lord has done it?
Surely the Lord God does nothing, without revealing his secret
  to his servants the prophets.
The lion has roared; who will not fear?
The Lord God has spoken; who can but prophesy? " [6]

One discourse is prose, phrased in abstract, technical terms. It
is the product of a scientific temperament and of deliberate
rational analysis. The other is a verbal expression of an intuition. It is a poetic production, making use of concrete and simple examples, rhythmic speech, vivid and colorful language.
Clearly, one is the symbolic expression of a scientific spirit and
the other is the speech of a poet. The contrast between these
two passages is typical of that between the Bible and the philosophical and scientific literature of the Greeks.

Of course, in the Bible one can find speech used ceremonially, expressively, directively, and logically. But these cases are
in the minority and they do not represent the over-all spirit
of the Biblical literature. Most Biblical speech is poetic, appropriate for communicating feeling, faith, and intuition. The
Bible *as a whole* is a poetic or dramatic production. The word
" poetic " is used here in a broad sense, not merely to denote
what we generally call poetry proper. Myth, legend, prophetic
utterances, poetry proper, and interpreted history are all
within the connotation of the term. All these symbolic devices
are products of the creative religious imagination. They set
forth in verbal symbols the intuitive seizures of meaning and
the value experiences of the human person. For purposes of
clarity, we cite some examples of the dominant poetic forms
in the Bible.

Myth:
   The Story of the Demigods (Gen. 6:1-4)
   The Story of the Tower of Babel (Gen. 11:1-9)
   The Stories of Creation, the Fall, and the Flood (Gen.,
      chs. 1 to 9)
Legend:
   The Stories of the Patriarchal Heroes (Gen., chs. 12 to 50)
   The Stories of Moses' Leadership (Ex., chs. 1 to 20)
   The Samson Stories (Judg., chs. 13 to 16)
Poetry Proper:
   The Psalms
   Job
   Lamentations
Prophetic Discourse in Poetry Proper:
   Amos
   Hosea
   Isaiah
   Nahum
Interpreted History or Drama:
   Joshua
   Judges
   Samuel-Kings
   The Synoptic Gospels
   The Acts

Whether mythological, legendary, prophetic, or dramatic history, the Biblical materials, suffused with religious imagination, have as their main function the communication of the grand intuitions of inspired spirits. The intuitions of an original creative act, of the inevitability of human sin, of the divine government of history, of the unique stature of Jesus, and of the exhilaration of redemption from misery — these are all symbolized in poetry. Who would desire it otherwise? Hardly anywhere in the Bible does one find much material that can be considered objective history or scientific description. Scarcely anywhere is there much material that has the character of a sophisticated, philosophical discourse. There is nothing comparable to Plato's *Dialogues* or Aristotle's treatises on metaphysics, ethics, or psychology. It was not a rationalistic Greek mind that produced the Biblical literature (though it was surely a Greek mind that produced the later Christian theologies).

The recognition of Biblical literature as poetry is of crucial importance for the interpretation of its meaning. On one side, we find the literalist, who wants to take the words of the Bible " as they stand " (he thinks he knows what they mean " as they stand "). His position is incredible. It is as absurd as that of a man who wants to interpret Dante's *Divine Comedy* literally. What results is chiefly superstitions and falsehoods. He simply fails to see what it is that he is dealing with: poetry. He operates on the false assumption that the Biblical materials are objective scientific and historical texts, that is, that they are language used in its logical function. On the other side, we find the rampant but unenlightened man of scientific disposition who is always looking for facts. He reads a little of the Bible and sees that most of what he hastily surveys is certainly not historical or scientific discourse. He therefore brushes the whole thing aside as the meaningless reveries of the childhood of the race. These two persons dispose of the Bible in very different ways. Curiously enough, they both are operating, however, on the same basic assumption. Both expect to find history and science expressed in logical language. They believe the texts will yield their meanings by means of a literal interpretation. Both fail to recognize that they are dealing with poetic texts and that they must use other means of interpretation for them than those employed in understanding Newton's *Principia*.

The Bible has a message to communicate. There is a Word behind the words. The language of poetry implies or suggests propositions, convictions, and truths. But one does not arrive at the truths expressed in poetry by an arithmetical process of adding literal meanings one to another in order to produce a sum. The meaning of poetic discourse is seized as much by the allusions of the metaphors, by sensitivity to suggestions, by the musical rhythm of the speech, and by intuitive rapport with the spirit of the writer as it is by the literal meanings of words. The Bible's Word is simply that there is a divine presence to be felt in life and that this God acts in history and nature to save men from misery, sin, and disillusionment. The Biblical texts express this intuition and faith among their various writers. They are offered to us in the most appropriate way in which such profound and exhilarating insights can be offered, namely, in poetry.

The Bible symbolized God anthropomorphically, that is, after analogy to the human person. Almost every student of the history of philosophy meets that notorious Greek, Xenophanes, before he has shuffled through a dozen pages of his textbook. He was among the first to take the poets of ancient Greece to task for their crude anthropomorphic speech about the gods.

God is one, supreme among gods and men, and not like mortals in body or in mind. The whole [of god] sees, the whole perceives, the whole hears. But without effort he sets in motion all things by mind and thought. It always abides in the same place, not moved at all, nor is it fitting that it should move from one place to another. But mortals suppose that the gods are born (as they themselves are), and that they wear man's clothing and have human voice and body. But if cattle or lions had hands, so as to paint with their hands and produce works of art as men do, they would paint their gods and give them bodies in form like their own — horses like horses, cattle like cattle. Homer and Hesiod attributed to the gods all things which are disreputable and worthy of blame when done by men; and they told of them many lawless deeds, stealing, adultery, and deception of each other.[7]

Xenophanes deserves credit for his desire to purify the conception of deity, for his inquiring spirit, and for his insight that religious ideas undergo a process of development.

From our earlier remarks, it is clear, of course, that it is entirely natural that poetic speech about God tends to be anthropomorphic. Anthropomorphism is a part of the technique of poetic expression. In great measure, this explains the presence of anthropomorphisms in the Bible. At this point it is important to give the ancient Hebrew credit for having been somewhat more intelligent than he is often reckoned to have been. We contend that the Hebrew writers recognized that their anthropomorphic speech about God was a matter of allusion. They were not, of course, completely emancipated in this respect. They cannot, however, have understood themselves as offering logical language. As someone has said, we ought not to think we are immensely more intelligent than the sages of the past simply because they happen to be dead. Moreover, it seems clear that the Hebrews' intuition of God was an intuition of deity as a person. It was, therefore, natural to allude to him by speech commonly used to describe the attitudes and actions of human persons. We maintain that the Hebrew was aware that his speech about God was allusion and metaphor. He was not as dense about the functions of language and their meanings as many modern literalists.

However that may be, the Greek philosopher and later the Christian theologian came to think that a sophisticated, technical vocabulary was more appropriate for talking about the nature of God. Their ways of speaking involved such terms as "infinite," "eternal," "omnipotent," "cause," "immutable," "substance," "unity," etc. The basic terms of the classical theological vocabulary were abstract terms, designating abstract conceptions. The vocabulary of the Bible is, however, comprised of concrete, vivid, anthropomorphic terms. God hears, sees, feels, becomes angry, is gracious, and so on. The question to which we come is very simple. Which set of terms is more meaningful? We can entertain some sort of idea of what it might mean for God to see, hear, be compassionate, or be irritated, because we know these actions and attitudes in terms of our relations to other persons. On the other hand, the abstract vocabulary of theology is for the most part meaningless. (For one thing, most of the terms are negative, expressing our ignorance rather than our knowledge.) If, in the interests of a meaningful religion, one had to choose between the two vocabularies, he must on semantic grounds select the Biblical vocabulary, however naïve it may sound. One prefers to have some meaning, crude as its verbal dress may be, rather than to have no meaning dressed in elegant speech. Xenophanes to the contrary, the Biblical speech about God must be preferred on the very simple, logical basis of meaningfulness. It must be remembered, however, that the meaning of Biblical speech is communicated through poetry.

Chapter X

The Delusion of Grandeur

The history of philosophy in the West is the celebration of the grand misapprehension that man is essentially a rational being. From the time of Pythagoras, Plato, and Aristotle until the nineteenth century, almost every prominent thinker in science, philosophy, and religion was moved by this lofty conceit. As a result, from beneath the masks of our philosophies and theologies, the specter of a naked intellect now peers out and mocks us. It was only an occasional solitary, rare spirit who recognized that the title " Homo sapiens " was a disastrous misnomer: a Pascal or a Kierkegaard, a Nietzsche or a Marx, a Rousseau or a Schopenhauer. This sovereign idea also exercised its power over much of the history of Christian theology, though some Christian thinkers escaped complete subjugation to it by occasionally reading the Bible.

Let us caricaturize the human situation.

And it came to pass that, after the Lord had filled the earth with living creatures, the strongest and most distinguished of the beasts gathered together to reflect upon their pre-eminence. The elephants were all gathered together in one place. And one opened his mouth and said to the others: " Indeed, we are the most blessed of all the beasts. For has not God given us dominion over the others? " They all gave agreement by a nod of their heads and a twitch of their impressive ears. And another said: " It is true — we are stronger than all other creatures and can grind them into the dust of the earth. But what is the secret of our power?" The first spokesman answered, saying: "Surely you cannot fail to see. It is our long, strong, and agile trunks that set us apart and above. Henceforth we have a name for ourselves — *Elephas proboskidos.*" And it came to pass that the wise of the herd began to say to one another, "The essence of elephant is trunk-ness." Soon the whole herd was not so much saying it as shouting it, without moderation in either thought or volume. The spirit fell upon them all, and all the young of the herd were diligently taught this doctrine. So it has been unto the thousandth generation that every normal and socially acceptable elephant is firmly persuaded that he is basically a proboscis. And any who sense that there is more to them than a trunk are promptly stampeded off the stamping grounds. And it has come to pass that most have now forgotten that there is anything behind their noses.

Man is a rational animal. He can solve some of his problems by mental trial and error and thus conserve time and energy. This simply means that he has a peculiar tool for dealing with his problems, the intellect, just as the elephant is equipped with a striking tool for life, the trunk. It is fallacious to infer that since man possesses the power of intellection, therefore he is *in essence* a rational being. Intellection is but one function or aspect of the whole person. Unfortunately, many great philosophers, scientists, and theologians whose thoughts have subtly fashioned our present estimate of ourselves all but forgot that man had anything beneath the top of his mind. We do not indulge in a doctrine of misology. It is important to recognize that nature has provided man with the tool of reason. Moreover, it is necessary that man use that tool effectively in attempting to solve his problems. The tool is, however, not the person who uses the tool. The failure to preserve this distinction leads to all kinds of misfortunes and misapprehensions in human affairs. Everyone today takes a secret pride in the thought that he is basically a reasonable man, even though his neighbors are with few exceptions downright fools. He tries to forget the hidden animal powers that use the peculiar tool with which nature had provided him.

The misapprehension that man is essentially rational was born in the sixth century B.C. in the work of that unusual man, Pythagoras. As far as we know, he was the first who caught a vision of mathematics as a rigorous discipline of proof. He is famous for many things, including the idea that all things are numbers, the advice to abstain from beans, and the doctrine of the immortality of the soul. He developed a geometric method for symbolizing numbers and conceived that number (more generally, mathematics) was the key to the understanding of nature. By and large, modern science confirms Pythagoras on the latter suggestion. According to this scientific mystic, man was a number-reckoning creature. The human soul, or intellect, which is the faculty that deals with number, is therefore deemed so important that it must enjoy immortality. Its nature is indicated by what it handles, that is, eternal essences. It is a short step from this sort of thinking, of course, to the conceit that man is substantially or essentially rational. We are indebted to Pythagoras and his disciples for their work in mathematics and science, but we must take exception to the doctrine of human nature that was implicit in much that they had to say about these disciplines.

Plato, whose thought was influenced by the Pythagoreans, helped further to foster this conceit. According to him, one of the chief functions of the soul was intellection. All knowledge was gained by the intellect's intuitively seizing abstract ideas and relating these ideas to one another logically. The good life was one in which the body and lower passions were ordered and directed by reason. Reality was an orderly arrangement of eternal, unchangeable, perfect structures or archetypes, which were the forms comprising the foundation of the class-structure patterns in nature. That is, ultimate reality was fashioned in the image of the abstract concepts that the intellect entertained. We now have, for the first time in history, a full-blown theory in which man has created all things in the image of his exalted conception of himself. This perspective is partly quali-

fied in Plato. What he had to say about love and beauty indicates that he recognized that there was a secondary, alogical
aspect to the soul. In Plato, as in Pythagoras, the dominant
doctrine of man found its inspiration in mathematics and logic.
One of the two chief studies in the curriculum of the Academy
was pure mathematics.

Plato's pupil, Aristotle, confirmed the West in the conceit
about human rationality. He judged that the human soul was
an active intellect. It is this faculty which distinguishes man
from other creatures. It is the active intellect alone which is
immortal. Reason potentially possesses all truth. The forms or
patterns of things are realized without error in the intellect.
Knowledge results from relating these abstract concepts to one
another according to the prescriptions of logic. The categories
with which the intellect operates — for example, substance, ac-
tuality, potentiality, and cause — represent metaphysical structures and relationships. The intellect rehearses in abstract
concepts the actual structure of ultimate reality. Aristotle is apparently reluctant to confess that reason is limited in any respect. Man as man is intellect. Schopenhauer called this the
" ancient and universal radical error," the " enormous first lie."
The seeds of this conceit were planted by Pythagoras, nurtured
by Plato, and came to fruition in Aristotle. Unfortunately, the
plant was a perennial one with prodigious powers of reproduction. Consequently, even today the garden of human intellectual and religious affairs is overrun with this hardy plant. We
cannot trace here all the main steps in its genealogy.

Let us try to state the nature of the fallacy we face. Mathematics made its appearance among the Greeks. Mathematical
demonstrations are majestic in their simplicity and impressive
in their elegance, rigor, and consistency. When one compares
the clarity and certainty of mathematical concepts and demonstrations with the complexity, coarseness, and confusion of
sensory experience, he cannot escape the feeling that in mathematics truth has clearly dawned in the human mind. It is
easy to understand that when the mind has produced such

elegant fruit, man will judge, first, that the intellect is the pre-eminent and divine element in man and even that man qua man is intellect and, secondly, that the necessity and rigor of mathematical relations are evidence of a certain apprehension of truth. In other words, validity is mistaken for truth (cf. Chapter VI). Thus, Pythagoras prophesies that all things are number. Plato fashions an eternal realm in the image of a mathematical system. And Aristotle insists that the intellect links man to the Prime Mover and that man is essentially rational. It was an overwhelming admiration for mathematics, combined with a misunderstanding of its function, that produced the conceit that man is essentially rational.

This prejudice, completely foreign to the Hebrew and the early Christian mind, entered significantly into the Christian tradition in the works of Clement of Alexandria and Origen (second and third centuries), who were Neoplatonists in philosophy as well as Christians. The Platonic realm of forms, now understood as dynamic rather than static, was incorporated into the concept of the Logos, which was elevated to a position of theological eminence just below God the Father and was identified with the Son. In Augustine (354–430) we discover the Neoplatonic conceptions of God as transcendent source of reality and goodness and of the human soul as distinctly rational warring with the Biblical views of God and man as personal wills. The early fundamental creeds of Christendom were a product of the vocabulary and spirit of the Greeks rather than of Jeremiah and Jesus. Plato and Plotinus were Christianized in the work of Augustine; Aristotle had his heyday in that of Thomas Aquinas. In almost every century from the fourth through the fifteenth, a Jesus of Nazareth would have felt thoroughly frustrated in this sort of rationalistic environment. The trinitarian formulation of the nature of God is a striking example of the alien world of abstractions. God is of one substance and three hypostates (persons), Father, Son, and Holy Spirit. Each person is of the same substance as God himself. The persons are co-eternal, co-equal, and consubstantial. The Son is eternally begotten of the Father, not created. The Holy Spirit proceeds (is not begotten or created) from Father and Son. It is clear that the heirs of Plato, Aristotle, and Plotinus can talk this way; it is incredible that the spiritual descendants of Isaiah, the psalmists, and Jesus would speak thus. The Christian creeds are, from one point of view, rationalizations in Greek philosophical categories of certain religious experiences among the early Jews and Christians. Those creeds were not, of course, chiefly interested in abstraction but in the interpretation of faith and certain historical events for the community of believers. The devices by which these religious experiences and facts were interpreted were, however, abstract concepts, the stuff with which the intellect works.

Later John Scotus (ninth century) insists that reason must be followed without reservation in matters of theology and philosophy: religious truths are rational truths. Thomas Aquinas (1225–1274) undertakes to prove the existence of God and the immortality of the soul by reason and to give an intellectual analysis of the divine nature. Anselm (1033–1109) submits a rational argument, not merely for the existence of God, but also for the necessity of the atonement. Abelard (1079–1142) takes up the tool of the intellect to test the intelligibility of almost every article of faith. These men operated on the axioms that man was essentially rational and that God was in essence rational. The human intellect could, therefore, rehearse in abstract concepts the very structure and operations of ultimate reality. Where they did not come close to the doctrine that man qua man is rational, they at least gave reason a pre-eminent position in the human creature and insisted that the intellect was competent to deal with metaphysical propositions. All of them would have appeared exceedingly ridiculous and conceited to an Amos or a Jesus.

Descartes (1596–1650), often called the father of modern philosophy, is famous for the invention of co-ordinate geometry and notorious for his resurrection of Anselm's argument for God. Anselm's argument is a brief but noteworthy example of the misapprehension that the human intellect can capture all sorts of victims, even God himself. In brief skeletal form, it runs like this: I have an idea of a most perfect being; perfection necessarily includes existence; therefore, God necessarily exists. In this formula, logic has taken God captive. With apologies to Pythagoras and all logicians, we may say that its force is about the same as the inference: all things are number; I understand number; therefore, I understand all things. Descartes started out in philosophy and science in an admirable fashion by doubting everything. As we begin to read his *Discourse on Method,* our hopes rise for a moment that once again the world will be blessed with a Socrates, an unrelenting skeptic, even unto death. But we are disappointed. Soon the man finds something absolutely certain: his own existence (*cogito, ergo sum;* for doubting the existence of the ego presupposes the ego for the act of doubting). From this axiom, he hastens to prove, beyond doubt, the existence of God and of an external world — and of each of these he gives a rational analysis. As in the cases of Pythagoras and Plato, the source of Descartes's inspiration was mathematics. He also succumbed to the same illness that seems to have beset most of the philosophers and theologians of the West — with or without the ministrations of logic, one must have certainty. For Descartes the distinguishing and fundamental feature of man was mind, thinking substance. After him, the celebration of this misapprehension continued with the help of Leibnitz (1646–1716) and Spinoza (1632–1677), for whom the controlling themes in philosophy and theology were the substantiality of mind, the metaphysical competence of the intellect, and the normative character of mathematical-like thought.

This short sketch of the philosophical festivities in the West may at least suggest how the spirit of Pythagoras and Aristotle hovered over these many centuries. In brief, our diagnosis is this: (1) The inspiration for this rationalistic spirit was the elegance, simplicity, and rigor of mathematical demonstrations. But mathematics was mistakenly understood to deal with things, physical or metaphysical, and therefore with truth. (2) From the idea that the intellect was the distinctive faculty of the human creature, men fallaciously inferred that they were *essentially* rational. Man as man is rational. (3) Because they thought mathematics dealt with reality, they judged that reality (or God) was rationally structured. The structure of ultimate reality corresponded to the logical categories and relations with which the intellect worked. The universe and ultimate reality were thus created in the image of man, understood as essentially mind. The human intellect was, therefore, assumed to be competent for metaphysical inquiries.

Psychologists sometimes advise us that among the several primary activities of the human creature we find inquisitiveness. Inquisitiveness has produced much that we prize in philosophy and science. It has expressed itself in Socrates, Galileo, Leonardo, Michelangelo, Newton, and many others of the illustrious company who have contributed to the development of a humane culture. Science and religion, properly understood, are two different ways in which human inquisitiveness is expressed. Our scanty survey of the celebration of the misapprehension about human nature suggests, however, a correlated idea. The desire for certainty is just as fundamental in man. Much of the history of philosophy and science can be characterized as a search for certainty. The yearning for final answers and certainty often proves to be more powerful than the desire for the adventure of continuous inquiry. Most men wish to be relieved of their doubts rather than deprived of the comfort that comes with the cessation of questioning. Nietzsche once wrote to his sister, "Here the ways of men part: if you wish to strive for peace of soul and pleasure, then believe; if you wish to be a devotee of truth, then inquire." [8] Only a few men have been able to sustain themselves as skeptical inquirers. Most finally give way to the enticing comfort that comes when one refuses any longer to ask critical questions. Those who are committed to the assumptions that man is essentially rational and that ultimate reality is rational are already provided with axiomatic ammunition to defend their lapse into certainty. Reason, they say, has brought them to final truth and no further questions need be asked. What a tragic sight it is to see, time after time, a Plato or an Aristotle, an Abelard or an Aquinas, a Descartes or a Spinoza, begin with the magnificent determination to doubt and inquire and then, because of a rationalistic conceit, lapse into a dogmatic defense of a system of absolute truths.

Descartes is the archetype of all those who celebrate the grand misapprehension. He apparently starts out to be a thoroughly skeptical inquirer, but he soon succumbs to the temptation and is found resting comfortably in some certain conclusions. Sometimes we even suspect that, in his case as in others, the thinker had his certainties to start with and only rationalized them with a system of argument. His doubt was artificial. He deceived himself and those to whom he gave his assurances of objectivity and skepticism. His doubt was one that he thought he exercised as a pure intelligence. It was not a doubt that was integral to the process of living as a whole person and to solving problems as a whole person.

This, then, is our cultural delusion of grandeur: man is essentially rational and he can gain certain knowledge of ultimate reality. Man refashions the whole of his world and the whole of himself in the image of what is only a tool with which he has been furnished for dealing with life's problems, the intellect. He develops a rigid, detailed picture of the world, with himself at its center. He finds Scriptural consolation for the conceit in the words of a psalmist: " O Lord, . . . thou hast made him [man] little less than God." [9] We cannot help recalling at this point Socrates' words to Euthyphro, the Greek theologian:

Good heavens, Euthyphro! and is your knowledge of religion and of things pious and impious so very exact, that, supposing the circumstances to be as you state them, you are not afraid lest you too may be doing an impious thing in bringing an action against your father?

And the answer of the dogmatist to this was:

The best of Euthyphro, and that which distinguishes him, Socrates, from other men, is his exact knowledge of all such matters. What should I be good for without it? [10]

Another aspect of this conceit is important for religious affairs. Early Greek ethics was rationalistic. The picture we have of Socrates shows that this idler of Athens held the opinion that living well was a matter of living intelligently: the unexamined life was not worth living. His advocacy of critical questioning, his tendency to think that moral living was wise living, and his idea that the cure of the soul involved cultivating intellectual and spiritual pursuits that released it from the limitations imposed upon it by the body — these were clues to a prejudice, not fully explicit in him, that man was not only basically rational but also basically good. In Plato and Aristotle, this thought is clearly expressed. Courage, justice, temperance, and all other virtues are reducible to knowledge. The good life is the life ordered by the intellect, acting under the inspiration and information it derives from the World of Ideas, Plato's mathematical heaven. Aristotle was just as adamant in insisting that virtue is the child of the intellect. This rationalism in ethics is expressed in the general Greek interpretation of moral evil or sin. The Greek's word for sin, *hamartia,* meant to miss the mark, as in an archery contest. To sin was to be unskillful in living. It was an error in judgment, a lack of skill, or a failure to think correctly about life's problems. The sinner was a man who could not think straight. To be saved from sin, then, did not require contrition or forgiveness; it required the enlightenment of the mind or learning. The sinner educated is the saint. The more intelligent a man is, the better he is morally. According to this reckoning, we should expect the doctor of philosophy to be the moral leader, which is substantially what Plato affirms by making the chief of his utopian state the philosopher-king. The Greek argument seems, therefore, to run this way: man is rational; the rational is good;

therefore, man is essentially good. This is optimism in one of
its most rampant forms. The reader may judge whether the
application of this logic in our culture has substantially allevi-
ated man's moral miseries.

As a matter of fact, by operating on the axioms of their essential rationality and goodness, men increase their own misery, anxiety, and disillusionment, for the facts of life never
bear out these idealistic hypotheses. Men always expect more
of themselves and others than they ever receive. Consequently,
they are always disappointed and frustrated. Nevertheless, it
is surprising how long men will obstinately cling to flattering
conceits in the face of facts that repeatedly refute them. By
and large, Western men today are Greek in spirit and outlook.
The conceits concerning man's essential goodness and rationality were smuggled into the modern era by the Christian tradition. They are flattering, and the human animal will buy self-
adulation at a preposterous price. Everyone likes to think of
himself as basically an intelligent and good man, even while he
torments his neighbor and lies secure and indolent in the certainty of his opinions.

No writer of the Old Testament was moved by these Greek
conceits. Only the writer of Ecclesiastes betrays something of
the Greek spirit, but he certainly did not share the particular
prejudices of which we have been speaking. For the Greek,
reason was the root category for understanding human beings
and their world. For the Hebrew, it was personality. The
Hebrew did not become obsessed with any part of his being.
He never let the part usurp the place of the whole. This is related to the fact that while the Hebrew distinguished himself
by his genius in religion and poetry, he was an ignoramus in
mathematics and science. Where in the Old Testament or the
New Testament does one find anything that reads like Aristotle's *Logic*, Euclid's *Elements*, or the scientific discourses of
Democritus? Nowhere. This is a very curious phenomenon.
Read comparatively Plato's *Phaedo* and Isa., chs. 40 to 55.
There is no escaping the striking contrast between the scien-

tific and the poetic spirits, between the man for whom intellectual analysis is of chief importance and the man for whom personal response is basic.

When we read the second account of creation in Gen. 2:4 to 3:24, we learn that " the Lord God formed man of dust from the ground, and breathed into his nostrils the breath of life; and man became a living being." This may be correlated with the statement in the first version (ch. 1:26-27) that God created man in his image. These affirmations indicate that while the Hebrew mind escaped the Greek conceits about man's being essentially rational and good, it shared with the Greek mind the persuasion that man had a place in the scheme of nature different from that of other animals. Man alone among the creatures was fashioned in the divine image. It required a special act of the breathing of the breath of life to make man a living being. He is made the aristocrat among the various living beings; but his intellect is not exalted, if indeed it is anywhere specifically mentioned. This serves notice that whatever other conceits informed the Hebrew mind, it did not entertain those involved in the delusion of grandeur.

As the story goes, it was because man was given special treatment in the creative act that he was granted dominion over all other living beings (Gen. 1:28) or given a rent-free lease on Eden (ch. 2:8). The expectation was that, having his life rooted in God by faith, man would live humanely and with proper humility and caution among other creatures. Had not God reckoned with the inertia of the dust of the earth? In any case, we shortly hear that, tempted by certain animal desires, by aspiration for a role greater than that of a creature, and by an indiscreet thirst for wisdom, the image sought to exist by itself. The creature rebelled against the Creator. By an act of parricide, man tried to usurp the sovereignty of God. In psychological terms, the myth about Adam's sin is a symbol of the parricidal act in the primeval horde and the guilt attached to that heinous offense. In any case, sin is here presented as personal affront. This is a sin such as additional les-

sons in mathematics and metaphysics will not cure. If one is
ignorant, he needs to be educated. But if he offends, dishonors,
and disobeys his master, he must be contrite and rely upon
forgiveness. When a man insults and dishonors his neighbor,
he does not go to him saying, " I will study differential calculus
and abnormal psychology and learn to be more skillful in dealing with you hereafter." The human creature does not parade
before us in the Bible as a naked intellect, but as a whole
personality.

The story of Genesis tells us that man was created in the
image of God and that he fell or degraded himself. That is,
man is at the same time both creative and destructive. The
symbol of the image represents the capacities in the human
creature for intelligent, humble, and compassionate behavior.
The symbol of the Fall denotes the capacities, existing side by
side with the former, for bestial, vicious, and arrogant behavior. The myth teaches that man is both humane and bestial
at the same time. The human creature is simultaneously creative and destructive. Both *Zoe* and *Thanatos* dwell in the
depths of the human heart. This is not so much a clever para-
dox as it is a plain statement of fact. The Hebrew mind was
uncomplicated enough to see the human being as he is: saint
and sinner at once. The failure of all utopias and, indeed, the
persistent ways in which men's hopes and plans for peace,
justice, and co-operative endeavor are shattered and thwarted
by war, pride, and ambition constitute a refutation of the hypothesis that man is essentially rational and good.

On the other hand, the abundant creative works of men in
art, literature, and science indicate that the hypothesis that
man is essentially bestial and destructive is likewise inadequate. Any acceptable doctrine of human nature must take
account of both sets of facts. The Biblical hypothesis of the
double-valued nature of man does more justice to the facts of
human experience than do the hypotheses of the optimists and
pessimists. In a sense, the Old Testament is an extended development of this idea. Jacob was reverent, but a little too shrewd

and avaricious to be a saint. Moses was a courageous leader, but given to streaks of unholy wrath. Saul was an eminent and courageous king, but frequently bullheaded, jealous, and vicious. Worthy later to be deemed the ancestor of the Messiah, David has his sins and errors painted with dramatic clarity. Even Jesus is portrayed, in the story of the temptation, as wrestling with the powers of evil and bestiality that lurked within the human breast. Hebrew history is a rhythmic reaffirmation of the intepretation of man set forth in Genesis, becoming ever more dramatic and insistent as we review the ranks of the heroes.

Adam is every man. Genesis tells us that no man is a saint, unscarred by jealousy, ignorance, lust, ambition, or violence. Likewise, no man is thoroughly bestial, beyond hope of rescue and rebuilding. Man is double-valued. This is a saner and truer picture of the human creature than either an optimistic Plato gives us or a pessimist like Thomas Hobbes offers when he declares that human life is nothing but nasty, brutish, and short.

The Biblical story of man contains a healthy recognition of human limitations. Estimating man always from the perspective of God, the Biblical writer was keenly aware of the finitude of the human creature. The Genesis story tells us that there are certain limits set for the creature, which man's obstreperous, mythological ancestor tried to overstep. The Biblical doctrine of sin is one way of specifying the finitude of the creature: no man is perfect or is capable of perfection in this life. The poet of Isa., ch. 40, voices a theme that runs through the whole gamut of Old Testament writings:

> Who has measured the waters in the hollow of his hand
>   and marked off the heavens with a span,
> enclosed the dust of the earth in a measure
>   and weighed the mountains in scales
>   and the hills in a balance?
> Who has directed the Spirit of the Lord,
>   or as his counselor has instructed him?

Whom did he consult for his enlightenment,
   and who taught him the path of justice? . . .
Have you not known? Have you not heard?
   Has it not been told you from the beginning?
   Have you not understood from the foundations of the earth?
It is he who sits above the circle of the earth,
   and its inhabitants are like grasshoppers.[11]

This is a more adequate characterization of the human situation than that given by the Greek thinkers who tell a story of the astounding conquests by reason of all things in the earth beneath and the heavens above. Man is limited in power of action, range of thought, sensitivity to values, and moral competence. To deny this is neither good science nor good theology; rather, it is insane reverie. The failure to face the fact of human finitude and to reckon with it in philosophy and theology results in the delusion of grandeur.

This is the Biblical therapy for the disease we have contracted from the Greeks: man is a person, not essentially an intellect; he is at the same time potentially a creative and a destructive animal; he can only healthily live out his life by a recognition of his finitude and of his need for orientation and power from a being beyond himself.

Chapter XI

The Human Prospect when God Is Dead

The twentieth century was directed to its place in one of the rear pews in the sanctuary of history by an usher who, to the communicant's embarrassment, did not so much whisper but shout: "God is dead! Today we shall have an anti-Christian service — and I am its herald!" Later, when the young church-goer learned that this enigmatic usher died while insane, he judged that this was quite understandable and proceeded promptly to forget him. And now it is only when he is faced with a catastrophe of stellar magnitude and calls to his aid the witches of Endor that this caustic apparition appears for a moment to speak again the same terrifying words. Nietzsche was a fusion of the spirits of Amos and Socrates. The result was comparable to a nebular explosion. This Elijah of a new anti Christian era is one of the most important and fascinating philosophers in the West.

Friedrich Nietzsche (1844–1900) is notorious for many things, including his violent attack on Christian morality, his doctrine of the superman, and his idea that the strong and creative man stands beyond good and evil. This misplaced Socrates has also been suspect because he has been falsely regarded as an anti-Semite and an early proponent of the high nationalism and military ambitions of the German Reich. This misunderstanding of Nietzsche can be traced mainly to the activity of his sister Elizabeth Förster-Nietzsche, wife of a leader of the German anti-Semitic movement, Bernard Förster. Walter Kaufmann's *Nietzsche: Philosopher, Psychologist, Antichrist* (1950) analyzes the Nietzsche myth and gives us a scholarly and engaging picture of the real Nietzsche and his thought. The philosopher is often discovered giving a distinctly prophetic and Christian criticism of the complacency and self-righteousness of the men and institutions of his day. Admittedly, he was frequently too caustic and vociferous. And when his illness began to move in and take toll of him, his inhibitions were lowered. There is little doubt, however, that Nietzsche was one of the great philosophers of all times, in spite of the fact that he did not follow the beaten paths of philosophical thought and formulated no system. As a matter of fact, his greatness lies precisely in his originality and his rejection of all block views of the universe. Indeed, Nietzsche was one of the very few men who maintained to the end the critical spirit of a Socrates. Most philosophers start with Socratic skepticism but eventually fall prey to certainty and the passion for a system. "Here the ways of men part: if you wish to strive for peace of soul and pleasure, then believe; if you wish to be a devotee of truth, then inquire," says the self-styled antichrist.

One of the curious but profound Nietzschean themes suggests another delusion that has developed in modern man's thinking about himself and his world. "God is dead, and woe is us!" This prophetic exclamation sounds like an inspired utterance of a Jeremiah who lacks the faith of Jeremiah. Nietzsche proclaims that God is dead and that he is the herald of an anti-Christian era that is dawning in human history. The philosopher feels like a solitary prophet on a torturous mission; he must be the first to declare the message and, being the first, he must suffer the hatred of men. No man has an easy lot who must preach disaster in the midst of complacency. God is dead — this curious news must reach the ears of men. We cannot discuss all the dimensions of this intuition here. We shall indicate one part of its meaning and try to develop this single in-

sight in order to lay bare a delusion to which Western culture
has been subject.

When Nietzsche proclaims that God is dead and that we
men have killed him, he is not preaching atheism. He was
agnostic: in the interests of intellectual integrity, he refused
to let his mind come to rest finally in any opinion. Atheism is
as much a firm metaphysical conceit as an unyielding theism.
The uncompromising believer and the firm denier have both
given up inquiring; that is, they both have died intellectually.
As one Danish thinker expressed it, holding an opinion firmly
presupposes too much intellectual complacency — it is like being married. To philosophize is to inquire continuously, to
experiment everlastingly, to be ever ready to call your presuppositions into question. In this sense Nietzsche is a rare philosophical spirit, an authentic heir of Socrates. Men who arrive
at opinions with certainty and formulate systems — for example, Aristotle, Aquinas, Descartes, Spinoza, or Hegel — are of
a different, less noble company.

The formula, God is dead, is Nietzsche's way of saying that
the modern world has so far advanced in the sciences as to
outrun and render antiquated the received Christian interpretation of God. The classical concept of God is no longer
commensurate with the world as it is now understood, though
that conception may have been appropriate for a pre-Coperni-
can world.

Before the fifteenth century men's interpretation of the
world in which they lived was quite simple. This view is associated with the name of Ptolemy of Alexandria (c. 127–151).
In brief, it held that the earth was the fixed center of the world.
About the earth, the sun, moon, and other celestial bodies revolved in epicycles. In the minds of most men, God and his
spiritual hosts resided in heaven *above* the strata of earth,
water, and air. The lair of Satan was *below* the earth's surface.
Here was a simple, comfortable three-story world, with man
squatting on his real estate at the center. Neither heaven nor
hell was far removed. Man must therefore walk with caution;

for invaders from heaven or from hell quite frequently put in their appearance, and they were to be treated with appropriate attitudes of reverence and fear. While man lived in this world with caution, he nevertheless felt "at home." He sat at the center of the scheme of things. The beloved of the race who had fallen asleep in the Lord were not far removed. The saints, angels, and the Lord of creation were all within calling distance and a long arm's reach. There was a certain comfort and security for a man in this Ptolemaic world. He lived in familiar surroundings, both physical and spiritual. It counted heavily with him that all things seemed to revolve about him and were directed largely to minister to his body and soul. He was at home in the world.

This feeling of being at home, based upon the current scientific explanation of the world, was strengthened by another factor. Man had learned well the ancient lesson that the welfare of his soul was a chief concern of God, the creator and redeemer of life. God had sent his only begotten Son into the world that he might suffer and die for the purpose of saving the human soul. The whole drama of redemption was focused upon man. The Lord had created man by a special act, setting him apart from other creatures over which he was to have dominion. The privileges of Eden were originally bestowed upon him. The whole epic of Scriptural history was a recitation of God's attempts, now by punishment and now by invitation to blessedness, to win back the wayward creature. Finally, to climax the drama, God himself came in human form to restore by sacrificial love the descendants of Adam. Man could look forward to a great day of the Lord when triumph would be spelled out in terms of men of faith being raised up into the celestial company of God's own chosen. The Christian drama of redemption centered upon man. The history and destiny of the race were the center of divine interest. Religiously as well as scientifically, the world revolved about man. The universe was not only *geocentric* but also *anthropocentric*.

The works of men like Copernicus, Galileo, Brahe, and

Kepler shattered the geocentric theory of the world's structure. It is true that some men before Copernicus, as far back
as early Greek times, had suggested a heliocentric theory of
the world system. There is a hint of it and of the earth's movement in the works of the Pythagoreans. Anaximander (sixth
century B.C.) even implied that there might be other worlds
besides this one of earth, sun, moon, and stars; and Aristarchus
(310–230 B.C.) clearly proposed a heliocentric theory. Others
contributed ideas to this early cosmology. It was, however, to
be overridden by the Ptolemaic theory. Copernicus' inspiration
was to be found, not especially in independent scientific inquiry, but in the writings of the ancients who had served these
suggestions to men only to have them spurned. Copernicus
and his scientific heirs produced a world view where the sun
stood at the center of the system and the earth was shoved
toward the margins of the world's structure. That it required
several centuries for such thinking to be accepted is testimony
to the reluctance of man to be dispossessed of his central position. But man was dispossessed — and God was evicted from
heaven, his third-story apartment. Man had a residence only
in the marginal areas of this new world and God seemed to
have been forced into the life of a celestial hobo. The Ptolemaic world view ministered to man's conceit that he must
surely have the seat of honor in the astronomical festivities. It
was a sharp and hard blow to his vanity and his dreams of
eminence to be thrust from the center of things. His sense of
being at home began to wither away. Now he was a stranger
in space. The terrifying distances and machinelike movements
of the planets, even of his own celestial vehicle, caused him to
tremble. His friendly, familiar environment had disappeared
as a dream, and he stood alone and unarmed against a world
that seemed to be little concerned for his hopes and aspirations.
We note Pascal's poignant expression of the thought that the
infinite reaches of space terrified him. The old God is dead in
such a world as this. The news of it did not, however, get
around quickly.

The Copernican revolution shattered the geocentricity of the world which had been built in the image of man's dreams of his grandeur. But the delusion persisted in another form as far as human sentiments, hopes, and values were concerned. The prejudice that man was at the center of things religious, social, and historical did not die — and it has not died yet. The general picture of the new, widened world held by men is still *anthropocentric*. To be sure (they say), the earth is an infinitesimal blob of mass in a huge solar system, which is but one small part of a nebula among other nebulae. To be sure, but man is nevertheless set apart from other creatures by a special act. He is still the focus of God's attention, and the whole drama of redemption simply says that God moves to minister especially to the human soul. The Protagorean spirit is still dominant: man is still the measure of all things. Therefore, we confront a curious situation. Man is not at the center of things — yet he is at the center. Man is not significant — yet he is most significant. We have here a kind of spiritual schizophrenia. Our sense of our insignificance in terms of our scientific understanding of the universe wars within us against our sense of importance in so far as religious prejudices go. The old God is dead; but still he is not dead.

Human pride was to be injured again. The dawning of the scientific hypothesis of evolution in the mid-nineteenth century struck another blow at man's usually high opinion of himself. This hypothesis had also been anticipated by a few early Greek and later philosophers. It did not gain a controlling position in human thinking until after the work of Charles Darwin (1809–1882). The publication of the hypothesis of evolution (1859, *The Origin of Species;* 1871, *The Descent of Man*) provoked much controversy and distress in religious circles, for it was estimated to be a major threat to the Christian persuasion that man is a creation of God. In part, it was a vision of the dispossessing effect of the hypothesis of evolution that prompted Nietzsche to declare without qualification, " God is dead."

The chagrin men at first felt upon learning that their species was naturally selected in an intricate line of development of life in a whole complex evolution of the physical world, of plant and animal life, was soon conquered. To be sure, man emerged, sometimes gradually and sometimes by mutation, over many millions of years from lower forms of life. Certainly, other species of animals underwent a similar development and some poorly equipped creatures were rolled under by the selective impetus of nature. But, so the transfigured prejudice runs, man is the culmination of this whole intricate process. The human creature is the most complex and sensitive in structure and is equipped with a tool no other creature has in like measure: reason. Man's peculiar facilities for behavior and communication have purchased for him an everlasting lease on the cosmos. The anthropocentric conceit of man is incisively expressed in his opinion that he is the culmination of the process of evolution. This conceit also involves the idea that the human group simply cannot suffer the fate of those species now called extinct. Onward and upward the process goes — and any further development in man must be an improvement of man as man. " Organic life, we are told, has developed gradually from the protozoon to the philosopher; and this development, we are assured, is indubitably an advance. Unfortunately, it is the philosopher, not the protozoon, who gives us this assurance." [12] This sort of thinking about man's exceptional position in the process of evolution proceeds, of course, on the assumption that the development of the cosmos is undergirded by a power or spirit at work to produce a moral and rational being as its end product. What idolatry is to be found, even among pious Christians, when it is assumed by them that the end of God's purposes is to be identified with a happy end of human life on this planet! Such an assumption not only testifies to human conceit but also to a narrow conception of God. Deity is made a prisoner by the chains of human pride. This is the principal idolatry of man. The Christian doctrine of redemption is idolatrous, then, to the extent to which it expresses the conceit that in the end God's purposes are to be identified with the preservation and beatification of man in the universe.

Now if one were to make a probable judgment about man's place and prospects in the evolutional history of the world on the basis of the evidence available, the best guess would be that man as a species will pass away in the midst of the fortunes and misfortunes of history. He will fade into the shades of the eons with Tyrannosaurus and Stegosaurus. If dinosaurs could have reflected upon their status and spoken about it, we can be sure they would have complimented themselves on being the eminent end product of evolution and have confused dominion with superiority and the immortality of the species. To express the question in theological vocabulary, may not the glory of the Creator and Sovereign of life require that the human species pass away and be supplanted by another reigning family? May not the purposes of God go beyond the happiness and survival of this one group of his creatures? Perhaps one day God will discover that the human experiment was a failure. Is faith in God strong enough to survive the shock that comes upon learning that his purposes outrun the survival and felicity of man? Unfortunately, in most religious circles it is not. The issue is laid bare, then, as to which is more important to man: his own happiness or the glory of God. The terror with which men flee before this prospect and the ridicule they shower upon it simply testify that they cannot entertain a grand conception of God as creator and one that does not identify God's purposes with their own good fortune. The aged deity they worship shortly dies, and the human prospect is an ignominious death. Of course, there is no other prospect than death, but it need not be ignominious.

The first conceit concerning man's place in the world, geocentricity, was shattered by the Copernican revolution. The second, anthropocentricity, remains yet to be thoroughly destroyed by another advance in human thinking. Just as there has been no return to Ptolemy, so there will be no resurrection of the anthropocentric view of the universe, once it has been buried alongside the geocentric perspective on the universe.

The old God is dead. It is imperative for the spiritual welfare of men that they raise their sights religiously and conceive God in more majestic and more subtle categories. The hypothesis of God must be formulated in terms that are commensurate with the rejection of the geocentric and anthropocentric theories of the universe and of history.

The Christian drama of redemption, which is focused upon man and his salvation, was a great factor in establishing and crystallizing the anthropocentric view of the universe. If the conceit is abandoned, then some thorough reconstruction of the doctrine of salvation will be required. The Christian tradition is not completely devoid of insights upon which a broader, less anthropocentric doctrine of salvation may be built. The idea of God as creator and sovereign of all life, of which man is but one aspect, furnishes an ample base upon which to build an understanding of God's dealings with his creatures in such a way as not to set man apart as a specially treated species. God can be understood as being equally concerned for the lives and fates of all living forms. Salvation can be conceived as a creative restoration of the healthy integrity of all of creation. Besides the doctrine of God as creator, another element in the tradition that is useful for the suggested reconstruction is that of the glory of God. This thought, mostly to the fore in the Calvinistic tradition, insists that God's activities are designed to serve finally, not human interests, but the deity's own glory, honor, or good pleasure. Let God be God! If a concept of God is worth having, let us not limit it with qualifications that subserve human prejudices.

One must look sharply these days to discover a man with a faith that confesses that God may employ the death of all mankind for a higher purpose. Perhaps this should not be the case. The doctrine of resurrection from death has been improperly restricted to men as individuals. The dismal prospect of the death of mankind may be the foreshadow of the cross that the species must bear in the interests of God's overriding, redemptive plan. It may not be the case that God will have to declare the human experiment a failure, as we said earlier, but that he will find that the race has, in its allotted time, completely served his purposes. The atonement of Christ does not relieve men as individuals from the penalty of death. We ought not to expect it to purchase a pardon for the race. It may, rather, be the case that the race effects a generic atonement on behalf of the whole of creation. The crucifixion of Christ is a sign, not merely of the death of each man, but of the death of mankind. And the myth of the resurrection is a symbol that indicates that the realization of God's purposes requires the crucifixion of the race. It is quite possible that the chief end of man is simply to glorify God, without enjoying him forever. Man's prospect is death. Our faith must be strong enough and profound enough to comprehend this. Let us not be overly anxious about the human prospect when the old God is dead. Our concern should be with the divine prospect when man is dead.

Chapter XII

What Science Does for Religion

As we remarked in Chapter I, a handful of generations ago
the relations between science and religion were handled by attempting to reconcile Genesis or other Biblical texts with the
prevailing scientific world view. One had to show, for example,
how the Biblical day of creation was equivalent to a hundred
thousand or a million years, or he found it necessary to provide a scientifically plausible explanation of how the flesh and
blood of Lot's wife was transmuted into a crystalline substance.
Unfortunately, this sort of conversation continues in a few dark
corners, despite the fact that the methods and subject matters
of science and religion are, as we have indicated, quite different.

Such attempts at reconciliation were frenetic activities occa-
sioned by a false problem and by a faulty understanding of
both scientific and religious activities and discourses. The partisans of the two camps wielded their micrometers and threat-
ened with their Bibles in vain, for religious discourse is a kind
of poetry and scientific utterances are not poetic. Consequently,
most of us fled from this field of contest long ago, if indeed we
ever entered it.

Recently, however, men conceived another method for handling the issue. Recognizing that science and religion are
different pursuits using incommensurate languages, they contended that one could nevertheless unearth certain postulates
and aims that are common to the two. We indicated earlier

what some of these common assumptions are.

Each discipline, for example, presupposes a unity or coherence in the universe, and each is in the business of articulating it in its own way. By its own method, each seeks also to draw upon the riches and resources deposited in creation in order to turn them to human advantage. Both of them seek to control conduct in order to introduce a greater degree of wisdom and sanity into the human situation. Both are engaged in the enterprise of rationalizing human experience under some sovereign abstract concept. And so on. This is the current, popular way of dealing with the relations between science and religion. It is generally deemed sound and respectable. It gives to each side its due and shows how reason and faith may walk hand in hand, at least at the level where each throws down its postulates. In our discussion thus far, we have, by and large, proceeded in this manner. Another perspective is, however, possible and viable. Moreover, it leads to some interesting results. The Scriptural passage concerning the departure of one evil spirit and the return of a platoon of demons to the refurbished home suggests, by an appropriate stretch of the imagination, what this point of view is.

The dark doctrine to which we refer is this: science performs one simple service for religion. It lays bare new sources of anxiety, evil, disaster, and peril. It continuously throws new and brighter light on the wide scope of destructive processes in nature. In short, science simply renews and refreshes the problem of evil. We are not describing what science does in general, but what it does for religion.

For every threat to life and health checked or eliminated by the modern miracles of science, seven new ones appear to spring up from the depths to harass man. Almost every gesture of the scientific hand to control a part of creation seems in that very movement to uncover the lair of unforeseen, awry, and distressing powers. When one old disease is conquered, we find ourselves facing several new adversaries of bodily and mental health. When new links of communication and transportation

are forged and slung from continent to continent, the tensions
in the human situation intensify, and the sour grapes eaten
anywhere set everyone's teeth on edge. Is the human situation
today any less perilous, any less subject to tension and anxiety,
or any stronger in its moral and religious dimensions than it
was one or two thousand years ago? Are we morally any better
off today than men were in the days when "there was no
king" in the land and "every man did what was right in his
own eyes"? On every side today, men cry out of their fear
and anxiety, "No!" Where one devil is exorcised by the scientific hand, seven are eisorcised.

Science performs the important — indeed, indispensable —
function of refreshing the problem of evil, which no authentic
theologian or philosopher can overlook, treat lightly, or make
less than central to his thought.

If the evil and deadly aspects of nature were not displayed
again and again in different and dramatic ways, some philosophers, theologians, and educators (who so urgently wish for
things to be good and rational) might think that they had
"solved" the problem of evil and that they could rest comfortably in their worlds of wish fulfillment. The conceit might
arise among them that they had succeeded in digging out of
the human heart the evil root planted in it or that, by their
Herculean efforts, they had decapitated nature, whose head is
Satan. As a matter of fact, not a few among us, enchanted by
the brave new world of the optimist's imagination, think that
the ancient problem of Habakkuk, Job, and II Esdras is no
longer ours. But because of the ineradicable evil root in the
human heart and on account of the demonic processes at work
in nature about us, no other sign is to be given to this generation besides the sign of Jonah.

Science never does wipe the face of Satan from nature. To
our consternation it only traces out in excruciating detail the
features of that enigmatic, threatening countenance. The chief
problem with significant consequences in the science-religion
arena is how a man will cope with death and disaster, whose

innumerable faces are revealed from generation to generation by scientific inquiry.

Science continues to tell an unfinished, essentially interminable story of the illimitable ways in which evil may befall a city. If one continues to have faith in God and confidence in his sovereignty, the nuclear question is the ancient one of Amos: "Does evil befall a city, unless the Lord has done it?" Why have so many philosophers and theologians answered, "Yes," whereas Amos answered, "No"? We give answer with Amos and the other prophets and give thanks to science for its refreshing of evil and for confirming the prophetic reply. By its renewal of the problem of evil in every generation, science shows that the words of Jesus are urgent and meaningful in every age — "An evil and adulterous generation seeks for a sign; but no sign shall be given to it except the sign of the prophet Jonah." Science does not rescue us from evil or even lessen in a significant degree its impact upon us. It simply refreshes and renews it. It provides no other sign. Indeed, it conspires with religion to raise up the single sign of the Master.

While logic and science offer no practical religious solution to the problem of evil, they can give some theoretical aid in arriving at a theological rationalization of it. It is generally recognized that the theological and philosophical problem of evil is made acute, if not insoluble, by the fact that, in the face of the evident evil and destructive aspects of nature, Christian thinkers have, by and large, been adamant in insisting that God, the Creator, is perfectly (infinitely) good and perfectly (infinitely) powerful.

Let us denote infinite goodness by the symbol g and infinite power by the symbol p. Each property can be logically negated. The negations can be designated by g' and p', respectively. Thus, g' means "not infinitely good" or "limited in goodness," and p' means "limited in power." Given two properties and the operation of negation, there are four and only four logical possibilities: gp, $g'p$, gp', and $g'p'$. The first alternative (gp) symbolizes the traditional Christian contention about God, which is refuted by the ubiquitous phenomena of evil. The remaining three alternatives are logically possible contentions about the properties of deity under which the problem of evil can be more easily handled. Each entails a concept of a finite god, limited in goodness, in power, or in both.

In passing, we remark that this logical approach to the question of the properties of deity can be used for formulating the possible diverse interpretations when one considers three, four, ... , or n properties. If we think of three properties, g, p, and r (say, rationality), there are eight possible interpretations of the divine nature, denoted by gpr, gpr', $gp'r$, $gp'r'$, $g'pr$, $g'pr'$, $g'p'r$, and $g'p'r'$. For four properties, there are $2^4 = 16$ possible understandings of God's nature. If someone judges that a two-valued logic (affirmation and negation) is too restrictive for deity, he may give the divine properties three, four, . . . , or m values, in which cases the logical possibilities to be considered are 3^n, 4^n, . . . , or m^n, where n is the number of properties one is dealing with. Clearly, the traditional theological texts have not thoroughly examined all the logical possibilities involved in the characterization of deity.

Returning to our examination of the divine properties g and p in the face of the problem of evil, the interpretations of God denoted by $g'p$, gp', and $g'p'$ offer, as we remarked, more realistic hypotheses about the divine nature than the classical alternative. The continuously refreshed, inescapable problem of evil requires us to limit either God's goodness, his power, or both his goodness and his power. From these alternatives, three theologies arise. They are different in significant ways from the received tradition.

We briefly describe only one of them here. One version of the theology symbolized by $g'p$ conceives God as the all-powerful, continuously creative source of the whole universe. Under it, we can preserve some meaning for the classical concepts of divine transcendence and immanence, if we think of the universe as " resting " in God as a part of his being. God transcends the universe in the sense that his being is "wider" than the bounds of the physical universe. Nevertheless, he is immanent, because the spatio-temporal world is a part of his being or an expression of a part of his being. He is omnipotent, for all the energies and processes in nature proceed from his creative being. In order to come to grips with the problem of evil in nature, we contend, however, that God is himself incomplete or has evil as a part of his nature (g'). Evil exists

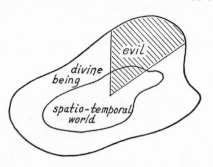

in the universe, because it exists first of all in him. The terrestrial struggles against it and against destructive processes in general are an expression of a wrestling by God himself with his own incomplete and unregenerate part. God is thus in process of self-realization. The groaning and travail in nature and in the human community are part of the greater redemptive contest that goes on in the divine nature itself.

One distinct merit of this hypothesis about God is that it lends itself easily to a broad interpretation of the redemptive process. As we remarked in Chapter XI, the traditional doctrine of redemption is needlessly and unfortunately anthropocentric. The drama of redemption centers on saving man. The whole of creation is, however, subject to disaster, error, evil, and destruction. All aspects of the universe — the inanimate domain, the plant kingdom, the animal world, and the human community — need to be redeemed from evils and limitations. The theology we advance here makes possible and calls for an

understanding of the divine redemptive activity as encompass-
ing the whole of the universe. Human redemption is but one
act in a more expansive, deeper process of salvation. God rec-
onciles to himself, not merely men, but the whole of creation.

Curious as this theological position may seem at first glance,
it stands closer to the Biblical utterances about deity and his
work than does the traditional theology of the Christian creeds,
which contends that God's power and goodness are infinite and
which, in spite of the facts of evil, refuses to ascribe it to
deity. The tendencies in the traditional formulations to make
God unlimited in power and goodness, to contend that he is
immutable, to dissociate him in one way or another from nature, and to ascribe to him infinitude in every respect came
into the tradition from the Greek philosophers. They were part
of the metaphysical heritage of Parmenides, of whom we shall
speak later. They were not an expression of the Biblical heritage. Among the testimonies of the Bible, God is the omnipotent creative source of all phenomena. The great prophets typically displayed no reluctance to ascribe evil directly to God.
"Does evil befall a city, unless the Lord has done it?" Moreover, the story of Jesus' temptation can fairly be interpreted as
a wrestling with an internal principle of evil in Him who is
deemed the unique manifestation of the nature of God. These
allusions simply suggest the nature of the manifold Biblical evidences that support, not the philosophical concept of God popular in our tradition, but a theological position close to that
designated by $g'p$.

The doctrine of the redemption of the whole of creation
that is entailed by $g'p$ is, moreover, commensurate with the
Biblical and Christian doctrine of the resurrection of the body.
Many theologians and philosophers have advanced concepts
and arguments related to the idea of the immortality of the
soul. As a matter of fact, most Christians today seem to believe
in a doctrine of the soul's immortality rather than a doctrine
of the resurrection of the body. The concept of the immortality
of the soul is chiefly of Greek origin. It was derived from ideas

related to the conceit that man is essentially rational and good. Furthermore, it presupposed the axiom that the soul, or intellect, was separable from the body. Among the Greek philosophers generally, this immortal, separable soul was impersonal. The doctrine of immortality that entered the Christian tradition was, therefore, connected with a faculty psychology, with the conceit about human rationality, and with a perspective that was dense to the category of personality. It was a distinctly unbiblical concept and has, ever since, been an uneasy member of the community of Christian doctrines. One looks in vain in the Bible for clear testimonies to a doctrine of the immortality of the soul. In the Biblical tradition, the dead are raised; their souls are not preserved apart from their bodies. In the Gospels and The Acts, Christ is resurrected and ascends into heaven; his soul does not persevere in a life outside the body. This is a crucial part of the story of the crucifixion and resurrection of Jesus, and its message tells us that the popular persuasion about the immortality of the soul proceeds from non-Biblical sources.

Furthermore, the Apostles' Creed contains no confession of the immorality of the soul. On the contrary, it affirms, " I believe in the resurrection of the body." In sum, the distinctively Christian and Biblical commitment about the afterlife is expressed in the concept of the resurrection of the body, which entails the idea that God's redemptive activity is directed to the whole person, body, mind, affections, and other aspects. As Albert Schweitzer once said, the man in the parable of Jesus did not save the *soul* of the lost sheep — he saved the *whole* sheep. This concept is clearly involved in the $g'p$ theology that we have been describing. All that this theological perspective adds is that the doctrine of the resurrection should not be restricted to men but extended to all forms of being. The divine redemptive work saves the whole universe in all its aspects from subjugation to error and evil. Let Christians have the courage to advance the nuclear contention of the doctrine of the resurrection of the body. It leads to a theological position that is, at the same time, fortified by a logical analysis of the properties of the divine and supported by Biblical contentions. In several ways, then, the theological perspective we have been advancing turns out to be more authentically Biblical and Christian than the traditional theology, which argues for the infinitude, immutability, and perfection of God and which harbors anthropocentric conceits and narrow views of the redemptive process.

This simple, partial exercise in logical analysis indicates another of the ways in which the methods of science can constitute a ministry to theology and religion. Through the services of science, we can arrive at a grander conception of God, at an understanding of his intimate connection with the processes of nature, at a new position for handling the problem of evil, and at a broader, less anthropocentric concept of redemption.

By some new ventures in logical and theological analysis, men can comprehend that the universe that science describes and controls is the same domain that religious faith affirms to be the scene of a continuous creative and redemptive activity. Moreover, Christian thinkers and theologians can understand that God saves the whole of creation from limitations and evils. The human soul has no privileged position before God. Furthermore, as we suggested earlier, the divine creative and redemptive activity may go far beyond securing the survival and felicity of the human race. It is the glory of God that is being advanced in the travail of creation, not simply the interests and conceits of men. In certain ways, then, science can lead us to more majestic and more useful conceptions of God and of his activities in nature and in history.

Theology as well as science requires abstract concepts for expressing what it deals with. It must, however, stay in touch with reality (phenomena), just as science does, if its formulations are to be of any use to men. While factual data are not able to demonstrate the existence and nature of deity, we cannot, on the other hand, hold a concept of deity that is refuted by facts. The general topic of the relation of abstract concepts to factual data is, therefore, relevant to theological inquiries. We now devote some attention to it.

One of the notable features of the new science that emerged in the time of Galileo and Kepler was the fusion of mathematical deductions with a new emphasis on observation and measurement. Leonardo da Vinci, Galileo, Brahe, Kepler, and others proclaimed that scientific knowledge must be fashioned in face of natural phenomena and be erected on the solid ground of facts. Galileo required that the scientific enterprise begin with " sensible experiments." Leonardo observed that the sciences are futile if they do not originate and terminate in " observation."

At the same time, the flourishing of the new languages of modern mathematics, among which we find Descartes's coordinate geometry, provided these pioneers with new kinds of conceptual apparatus and deductive tools for expressing the laws of nature and for making accurate calculations. Leonardo was as insistent upon the use of mathematical demonstrations as upon beginning with observations. There is no true science without mathematical descriptions and deductions. Galileo maintained that nature is written in mathematical language. " Without mathematics I am blind," he asserted.

The dual accent on observation (facts) and mathematical formulation (abstractions) was one of the striking features of the scientific method conceived at the outset of the modern period. The method of the new science demanded a fusion of empirical and rational factors. It married abstractions to phenomenal data. Otherwise said, it combined intensional and extensional factors. Although the relationships between abstractions and deductions, on the one side, and observations and measurements, on the other side, remain to some extent a mystery, this fusion of the rational and empirical is a dominant feature of contemporary scientific method. The fact that certain problems and mysteries lie hidden within it may be made clear by reference to the problem of induction by simple enumeration — the question as to when, or how, in counting black crows, we can affirm the universal statement, "All crows are black." As Bertrand Russell has said:

> The problem of induction by simple enumeration remains unsolved to this day. . . . The thing that is achieved by the theoretical organization of science is the collection of all subordinate inductions into a few that are very comprehensive — perhaps only one. Such comprehensive inductions are confirmed by so many instances that it is thought legitimate to accept as regards them, an induction by simple enumeration. This situation is profoundly unsatisfactory, but neither Bacon nor any of his successors have found a way out of it.[13]

In spite of the unsolved problems rooted in this mystery, it is clear that modern science is based on facts and uses facts to corroborate its theories, while it expresses its laws in mathematical formulas that are strictly universal propositions. The empirical side of science says in existential spirit, "Some crow is black," and the rational side proclaims in high abstractions, "All crows are black."

What is the logical structure of a modern scientific system? First, let us note that an observation is expressed logically in an existential proposition such as, "There exists an x such that x is wet," $(\exists x)W_x$, or "There exists a cat which is black," $(\exists x)C_xB_x$. Such a report has, as the scientist says, existential significance. The abstractions in it are low-level ones. In any case, it involves no commitment about all members of a class with respect to the property W or with the respect to the properties C and B. Secondly, a scientific law expressed in mathematical form is by its very nature strictly universal. It has the logical form, "For all values of x, if x is a planet, then x has an elliptical orbit," that is, $(\forall x)(P_x \supset E_x)$. Such a statement is about all members of a class. It involves high-level abstractions. It is highly intensional. Theological propositions are, of course, of this character also.

A modern scientific system is, as we remarked, a combination of universal laws and reports of observations (generally, statements of initial conditions). Its logical structure, then, appears to be a set of premises that can be written symbolically in this way.

LOGICAL STRUCTURE OF A SCIENTIFIC SYSTEM

$$
\left\{
\begin{array}{l}
\left.
\begin{array}{l}
(\forall x)(B_x \supset C_x) \\
(\forall x)(D_y \supset E_y) \\
\cdot \ \cdot \ \cdot \ \cdot \ \cdot \ \cdot
\end{array}
\right\}
\begin{array}{l}
\text{strictly universal propositions} \\
\text{high-level abstractions}
\end{array} \\[2em]
\left.
\begin{array}{l}
(\exists x)(J_x \cdot K_x) \\
(\exists y)(L_y \cdot M_y) \\
\cdot \ \cdot \ \cdot \ \cdot \ \cdot \ \cdot
\end{array}
\right\}
\begin{array}{l}
\text{existential propositions} \\
\text{low-level abstractions in reports}
\end{array}
\end{array}
\right.
$$

That is, the structure of such a system is a combination of some strictly universal statements and some existential statements. Taking these statements as premises, the scientist makes deductions and then proceeds to test whether or not his deductions are corroborated by the facts.

Assuming that this is a fair picture of the conceptual skeleton of a modern scientific system, we can call attention to several of its significant features.

First, suppose a proffered scientific system (or theological system) is comprised solely of strictly universal statements of the form $(\forall x)(B_x \supset C_x)$. That is, the system contains no existential propositions, reports, or statements of initial conditions. It is clear that deductions can be rigorously made from the system. Whether or not these deductions are interminable is a moot question that we need not discuss here. In general, however, a lengthy and logically secure process of mental maneuvers is possible. But apart from their validity or precision, what is their character? An examination of such a proposition as $(\forall x)(B_x \supset C_x)$ leads to an interesting conclusion. In the case of this sort of proposition, the implication is logically true even if there exist no members of the class over which x ranges. Mathematicians refer to this situation by saying that a formula is vacuously satisfied. For example, the proposition, "For all values of x, if x is an integral square root of 2, then x is a prime number," is true simply because there are no members of the class "integral square roots of 2." In other words, a knowledge of the form of the universal proposition $(\forall x)(B_x \supset C_x)$, or even of its truth, does not tell us whether or not we are talking about anything in particular. Whether we deal with scientific or theological statements that are strictly universal, we may very well be talking in empty concepts. By means of high abstractions or by the use of strictly universal propositions alone, one can elaborate a theory, but unless some existential assertions bring us in touch with facts, the theory has lost touch with reality. This is true, of course, in the case of sets of mathematical formulas in which scientific concepts and laws are expressed. It is also true of theological propositions. The theologian wins a hollow victory for his assertions, then, if their truth rests upon their being empty of meaning and irrelevant to the phenomenal world.

Secondly, what situation do we confront if a proffered system is made up exclusively of existential propositions? It consists, in this case, of a set of unconnected, self-contained reports. The only abstractions or relations in the system are those minimal ones required to make the reports meaningful. Consequently, no deductions (or at least very few) are possible. Little progress in thought is possible. Moreover, since the principle of induction by simple enumeration is unwarranted (the inference from "some" to "all" is logically unjustified), we cannot raise up from the set of existential propositions itself any high-level abstractions or universal laws for relating the reports. In this case, then, we know that we are talking about something — we are in touch with phenomena — but we cannot do anything with the system by way of guiding future conduct. Such a system cannot achieve the goals of science to which we referred earlier, for example, that of the rationalization of the world. Guidance of behavior and, indeed, knowledge itself require the apprehension of relations among things, abstractions of a level higher than those in reports, and logical deductions. These, in turn, demand universal propositions for their expression.

In sum, where a conceptual system is made up exclusively of universals, we can make deductions but cannot know whether or not we are in touch with reality. When it is constituted solely of existentials, we are in touch with reality but cannot make many deductions or much progress in thought and control of the world. In either case, adequate guidance of conduct is impossible. It is clear, therefore, that the requirement in modern empirical science for a scientific system containing some universals and some existentials is absolutely necessary if we are to have anything other than either speculative abstractions or unrelated reports. It is also a necessary condition for a scientific system that is to guide behavior in the direction of controlling the world. Modern science's power over nature and its use of prediction rest upon the happy fusion of universal and existential statements.

The remarks we have just made about the structure and usefulness of a scientific system are also applicable to a theological system. Theological propositions generally are very high generalizations or strictly universal statements. A theological system requires them if it is to be fertile and meaningful. But it also requires statements that are related closely to the facts of human experience and to natural phenomena if it is to be applicable to life and not be a skein of abstractions floating free from the world. Theology as well as science seeks to advance an understanding of the world and to exercise control over human behavior. It is therapeutic as well as theoretic. It proposes to formulate and advance abstractions in order to guide human conduct into the paths of sanity. One of the sets of facts to which theological abstractions must significantly relate themselves is that which specifies the principalities and powers of evil in nature. Failure to fulfill this condition is likely to result in our theological concepts being empty and useless. This is one of the reasons why a serious consideration of the theological systems denoted by $g'p$, gp', and $g'p'$ is necessary.

What does science do for religion? It renews and refreshes the problem of evil. Thus, it makes the sign of Jonah perennially significant. In these ways, it indicates clearly that some other theological alternatives besides the traditional one are necessary. It goes beyond this. It also provides the mechanics of logical analysis for specifying these alternatives and for beginning to make an assessment of them in order to find a fertile and useful theological option. Science and religion co-operate in a therapy for men who are beset by misery, anxiety, and evil. They both point out the direction along which the human pilgrimage to sanity and humanity lies.

Chapter XIII

Life, Logic, and Faith

The pre-Socratic scientists and philosophers were a tribe of in-genious thinkers. Many of the dominant thoughts of the mod-ern age are to be found in germinal form in their works. Py-thagoras was a prophet of the power of mathematics. Thales, Anaximander, and Anaximenes were probably the first formu-lators of scientific hypotheses about the world's structure and functioning. The idea of the evolution of living beings is to be found in Anaximander, Empedocles, and others. The Pythag-oreans suggested that the earth was spherical and that it moved. The current axiom of science that beneath the seeming stability of the world all is in flux was explicitly set forth by Heraclitus. Empedocles understood that there was sex in plants, that the moon reflected light, that light had a finite velocity, and that there was such a thing as centrifugal force. Anaxagoras, who suffered the misfortune of bringing science and philosophy to Athens, suggested that the sun was a fiery stone and that the moon had mountains and valleys on it, an opinion that Galileo many centuries later discovered to be en-tirely too novel for his day. Leucippus and Democritus pro-duced a highly sophisticated and well-articulated atomic and mechanistic theory of the world.

A heliocentric theory of the celestial bodies, the concept of the existence of a vacuum, and the thought that all qualitative differences are reducible to quantitative differences were other ideas blustering about the intellectual world before the days of

Socrates, Plato, and Aristotle. Unfortunately, most of these ideas and suggestions were thrust off to the margins of the race's consciousness under the hypnotic trance induced by the Platonic and Aristotelian systems. And after the church leaders and theologians virtually canonized Platonism and Aristotelianism, these renegade thoughts were thoroughly ostracized. But, as is so often the case with repressed novel ideas, they were later discovered to be the most creative and fruitful of their era. The pre-Socratics were in many respects more ingenious thinkers than the lecturers and pupils of the Platonic and Aristotelian academies. This is true, despite the fact that certain of these protoscientists thought themselves to be gods. The history of science has seen two periods of intense creativity. The first was that of the pre-Socratic era; the second was that of the scientific age that dawned in the fifteenth and sixteenth centuries. Between the two, there intervened two thousand years of scientific mediocrity and stagnation.

One of the members of this early, unusual tribe of thinkers, Parmenides by name, is of particular interest to us. In great measure, this man is responsible for the subsequent misuse of logic and the peculiar and burdensome metaphysical systems under which men have labored ever since. Parmenides lived in Elea, in southern Italy, about 500–450 B.C. He was allergic to change. Earlier Heraclitus had contended that everything was in process of change. Parmenides thought nothing changed. It is not this curious doctrine itself which interests us, but the way in which the philosopher justifies it. His argument is based on the logical principle of contradiction.

Consider a growing thing, say, a plant. It appears to be changing. But the plant cannot be in process of change; for if it changes from one moment to the next, then it is different later from what it was before. It is not what it was. Hence, it is what it was and it is not what it was. Contradiction! — therefore, no change. Metaphysically speaking, the Real is *what is*. *What is* is unchangeable; for if it did change, then *what is* is what is not. Everybody can see that this is absurd. Consequently, the Real is immutable. By a like use of the principle of contradiction, Parmenides discovers that the Real is one, homogeneous, indivisible, uncreated, and indestructible. It is also transparent and spherical. All change and all the qualitative and quantitative differences we sense in our world are illusory. There is only the immutable, indivisible, eternal, homogeneous *what is*. If the testimonies of the senses contradict the force of logic, so much the worse for the senses. This is at the same time very insane and very important.

It is very important, first, because Parmenides gave a rather complete list of the attributes that were thereafter to be ascribed to a metaphysical substance. Subsequent philosophers and theologians were in general unable to escape the subtle thralldom of his recitation. Plato's Ideas, Aristotle's Prime Mover, the Christians' God, and Spinoza's Substance were all characterized by most of the Parmenidean properties. Parmenides set the fashion for metaphysical and theological thinking for at least a score of centuries.

Secondly, in Parmenides one discovers a man who is adamant about confusing words with things. A semantic error of tremendous significance is planted in history at this point. As a result, throughout the subsequent centuries philosophers and theologians operated on the axiom that if they were able to talk, they were therefore talking about something. It is curious that some semanticists today ascribe practically all the ills of the race to the heritage of Aristotle. They pick the wrong man as the source of the curse upon the race. Parmenides is the Adam of this polluted stream of intellectual nonsense and depravity. Aristotle only repeated, in systematic form, what he learned from his philosophical fathers and they from Parmenides.

Thirdly, the business of going all the way with the force of logic, even to the extent of contradicting the senses, is a testimony to the fact that Parmenides shared and fortified that delusion about the essential rationality of man of which we spoke earlier. There were no barriers beyond which the human intellect could not travel with confidence, exhilaration, and success.

One point suggested by the work of Parmenides deserves particular attention. No one can escape the thought that in Parmenides the laws of logic, especially the law of contradiction, are considered immutable, eternal truths, untainted by the dust of the earth. Moreover, after Aristotle wrote his treatise on logic, no sober man doubted that the gods themselves authenticated them and indelibly inscribed them on the human mind. Aristotelian logic reigned supreme in the West until the period of the rise of modern science. Its force is not completely spent even today. This idea of the immutability, eternity, and absoluteness of the laws of logic fitted in very nicely with the classical idea of the independence and substantiality of mind. The intellect was different from and independent of the physical structure of man. Logic was the tool of intellectual inquiry. Therefore, the laws of logic are not founded in human experience but in some eternal realm above and beyond the terrestrial world. This misunderstanding is still perpetrated by some textbooks upon the occasional student who elects a course in logic under the misapprehension that it will help him to make money. For example, when the law of contradiction is spoken of as self-evident or as intuitively apprehended, it is lightly suggested that it is not based upon anything as lowly as sensory experience.

The lesson taught now for some time by psychologists that mind and body are intimately connected indicates that this understanding of the status of logical laws is in error. Mind and body are two aspects of one functional whole, the person. Studies of so-called functional disorders and their origins make it clear that physical conditions have mental repercussions or correlates, and vice versa. Any science, theology, or philosophy erected on the assumption of the autonomy of the human intellect or soul must be overhauled. Granting that there is an indissoluble and intimate relationship between body and mind, one should be able to find something in human experience that corresponds to or gives rise to the laws of logic.

We choose one of these laws for consideration. It is the law of contradiction, of which Parmenides made such rampant and disastrous use. Our question is, Is there anything in man's behavior as a user of symbols and as a physical organism to which the law of contradiction may be reasonably traced? Is there an empirical basis for this fundamental law of the formal sciences of logic and mathematics?

The law of contradiction can be expressed this way: not both A and not-A. It says that one cannot both assert and deny a property of an object at the same time and in the same respect. "The coin is copper" and "The coin is not copper" are contradictory. "All metals are solids" and "Some metals are not solids" are also contradictory. Similarly, "$X = Y$" contradicts "$X \neq Y$." The law of contradiction simply says that you cannot both have your cake and not have it at the same time.

In another place, the writer related the meaning of the law of contradiction to the simple mechanics of the process of naming and to the need to preserve the distinctions among names for things. This is one way of connecting this logical law to the exigencies of human experience. He also argued that the three basic laws (identity, excluded middle, and contradiction) are essentially one.[14]

Studies of the conflict behavior of animals indicate that there is an empirical basis for the law of contradiction and other logical principles. Let us speak to a specific point. One suggestive report of such studies is made by Neal E. Miller under the title "Experimental Studies of Conflict Behavior," in *Personality and the Behavior Disorders*, edited by J. McV. Hunt. Miller shows that conflict behavior is produced in a rat when the animal is both attracted and repulsed by the same goal. This approach-avoidance competition may be observed, for example, when a rat is driven by hunger to approach a feeding trough but is repulsed by fear of a shock that it has received at previous feeding periods. The animal both wants to approach the goal and does not want to approach it. When the

drives are intense enough and are balanced, a state of stable
equilibrium occurs and overt symptoms of a "neurosis" can
be observed.

Similarly, when an animal finds itself in a situation where it
has before it alternative courses of action, all of which it is
driven to avoid, conflict behavior results. If there is an escape
path, the animal can flee from the several dire alternatives and
avoid distress or anxiety. This avoidance-avoidance competition is an interesting empirical correlate to the logical dilemma.
One form of the dilemma is: either A or B; if A, then X; if B,
then Y; therefore, either X or Y.

These experiments with animals are simply carefully controlled and measured investigations of phenomena quite obvious in human behavior situations. Conflict behavior of the
approach-avoidance or the avoidance-avoidance type exhibits
itself in the human creature in the symptoms of anxiety,
despair arising out of frustration, withdrawal from the external
world, or undisciplined, frantic responses. If the conflict situation is not broken down, neuroses and psychotic maladies are
likely to result. It is not unknown for some persons to be so
thoroughly frustrated and overwhelmed with despair or anxiety that they take their own lives or deteriorate physically.
Conflict behavior bars healthy mental and physical development.

In a conflict situation, a decision is required if the animal
is to preserve its health or life. But, in general, no decision
can be made, because any decision will bring disastrous consequences. Certain problems of great magnitude must be
solved if life is to continue. The solutions of these problems
require, however, decisions or choices. When no decision or
choice can be made, the animal withers away in the inescapable equilibrium of indecision and frustration. The approach-avoidance situation may be described this way: not
both approach to the goal and withdrawal from the goal. The
avoidance-avoidance complex can be described thus: not both
withdrawal from this goal and not approach to that goal (in

the case where there are two alternatives, each of which prompts withdrawal). We suggest, then, that in such necessities of life as decisions in conflict situations we find the empirical foundation for the law of contradiction. "Not both X and not-X" is an abstraction at the level of conception and verbalization of the inescapableness of such decisions if one's life is to be healthy or even to continue at all. It expresses the "truth" that you cannot both have X and not have X without life being vitiated by despair and anxiety and deteriorating under the death-dealing impact of indecision. In this respect, logic, which is in part based on this law, is not so impractical a discipline as it is often made out to be. It does not follow from this, however, that one is on the way to schizophrenia if he does not agree with Parmenides' metaphysics!

Someone may ask, "Why is it, then, that a person who is not aware of these considerations concerning conflict behavior readily accepts the law of contradiction as a postulate of thought when it is first explicitly proposed?" In part, this is due to the fact that the law has been implicitly present in the mechanics of naming things, a process in which he has been involved from his earliest years. This immediate acceptance is, moreover, a matter of recognizing in distinct and clear form a principle that has been for a long time at work in one's behavior and of which he has heretofore only been half-conscious. The necessity of decision or choice in problem situations and the correlation between anxiety and illness and the stable equilibrium of conflict situations are made painfully clear to a person from early childhood. They become a part of the fiber of his life. For behavior to conform to this "logic of life" becomes as natural and habitual as withdrawal from some source of pain, such as fire. Man senses the logical exigencies of life in an animal-like fashion, though they never have been clearly conceived in consciousness. When the conceptualization of them is distinctly set forth, his reaction is, "To be sure, I knew it all the while — it is self-evident."

We suggest, then, that logic — the morphology of intellectual or symbolic operations — is not related to religion in the manner in which Parmenides and philosophers in general thought it was: as a method for giving rational demonstrations for metaphysical and theological doctrines. It is related to religion in terms of its being a set of abstract expressions for the structures of certain behavioral situations and in terms of its being a set of guides for conduct. As a set of generalized rules for problem-solving, logic provides controls for living healthily, that is, living without being seriously impaired by anxiety, despair, and the other results of conflict behavior.

As we observed earlier, religion too is a way in which men deal with their problems. It is interested in cultivating the integral, compassionate, and purposive life. It is a method that enables a man to come through problem situations without being overwhelmed with despair and anxiety. Religious faith as an intuitive seizure of the reality of God or the concept of God as a sovereign idea in consciousness gives an inextinguishable and unvarying focus to life. The hypothesis of deity and faith in God orient the processes of life — they serve to integrate and strengthen the person. They give a man a sense of power and purpose that equips him mentally and physically to cope with his problems and to triumph over indecision and anxiety. The idea of God is a hypothesis employed in the problem-solving process. As such, it is a guide for conduct in the same way as the laws of logic are guides for conduct.

Both science and religion attempt to fortify the human person for effective and successful conduct in the face of life's problems. Living scientifically and living religiously become one and the same thing. Logic and faith co-operate to promote health and sanity among men.

What are the mechanics of the Parmenidean mind, whose bias differs radically from what we have been suggesting? Earlier we described the hypothetical status of religious ideas. The religious man uses his ideas as the scientist uses his hypotheses — as guides for behavior. Religious ideas are abstractions, subsisting above the concrete situations and prob-

lems of life. Now we have asserted that the laws of logic are
similarly abstractions from life situations. Both types can be
and should be used for the direction of conduct. What has
happened in the case of Parmenides and his heirs is that the
one set of abstractions (the logical ones) is used to rationalize
the second set of abstractions (the metaphysical or theological ones). The resulting system is thoroughly divorced from
reality and from concrete life situations. This abstractness and
absence of contact with the facts of experience is clearly evident in Parmenides' metaphysics. Moreover, since he mistook
validity for truth, these abstractions were conceived to be
specifications of what is ultimately real.

This diagnosis of Parmenides' mental illness is also applicable to the similar illness in the majority of Western philosophers and theologians. In their works, we find metaphysical
and theological abstractions rationalized by logical ones. Some
of the simpler examples are the traditional ontological, cosmo-
logical, and teleological arguments for the existence of God as
presented by Anselm and Aquinas. The result is a highly elusive and highly articulated dream, divorced from the facts of
human experience and nature. This dream appears in the
minds of those who have forgotten, in their doctrinal raptures,
that logic, the factual sciences, and religion are rooted in human experience and are designed to be guides for human conduct.

The spirit of science, of logic, and of religion is the spirit of
inquiry. We have characterized life as a process of problem-
solving. The techniques of the factual sciences are designed to
control and manipulate nature and life. They seek understanding in order that they may direct human conduct. Their
quest is never brought to a halt in any certainty. Their judgments and laws are reckoned as hypotheses, which admit
doubt and permit further research. Among these sciences, hypotheses are held only as long as they are effective in the
quest for more knowledge and greater control over the world.
Logic and mathematics, the formal sciences, are not founded

on any absolute and eternal verities. They are sets of abstractions from the stuff of experience. These abstractions are also used to direct human conduct into healthy paths and to give men more effective control over themselves and their world. To employ the criteria of logic in thought is to be engaged in a quest for a more vital, healthy life. Furthermore, to live under the impetus and inspiration of a religious faith is to be engaged in a quest for greater and greater integrity, sanity, and felicity in life. It is an unending process — and it finds no intellectual terminus.

Science, logic, and faith are all methods of inquiry. None is dogmatic in spirit. None terminates in certainties. The spirit and method of all three, properly conceived and exercised, is the spirit and method of doubt. All three move from theory to therapy, intending to make the human situation one of greater sanity, integrity, compassion, and humility.

Inasmuch as science and religion share a spirit of inquiry and an attitude of humility in the presence of truth, effective communication can exist between them. Since both are directed to fostering among men a greater understanding of their world and a greater measure of physical and spiritual health, they have a common mission. On the basis of the compatibility of the logics of inquiry expressed in them, the Christian faith can address itself meaningfully to an age whose outlook has been largely fashioned by modern science. Logic is the language by which men of faith and men of science can communicate in order to advance jointly humane ideals and behavior in the human community.

Notes

1. F. W. Snyder and N. H. Pronko, *Vision with Spatial Inversion* (University of Wichita, 1952).

2. The word "mind" is a loaded term. It has certain substantive connotations that we do not accept. Nevertheless, it is used here for the sake of simplicity. It denotes certain facilities of the person, such as remembering, inferring, comparing, imagining, etc.

3. W. A. Kaufmann, *Nietzsche: Philosopher, Psychologist, Antichrist* (Princeton University Press, 1950), p. 325.

4. The contrast between the Hebrew and Greek minds is profoundly and excitingly set forth by Thorlief Boman in his *Hebrew Thought Compared with Greek* (tr. by Jules L. Moreau; The Westminster Press, 1960).

5. Aristotle, *Metaphysics*, 1013ª24–1013ᵇ10, in Richard McKeon, *The Basic Works of Aristotle* (Random House, 1941). Used by permission of Random House, Inc., and Oxford University Press, Inc.

6. Amos 3:1-8.

7. Milton C. Nahm, ed., *Selections from Early Greek Philosophy* (3d ed.; F. S. Crofts and Co., 1947), p. 109. Used by permission of Appleton-Century-Crofts, Inc.

8. Kaufmann, *op. cit.*, p. 21. Used by permission of Princeton University Press.

9. Psalm 8:1, 5.

10. Plato's *Euthyphro* in *The Dialogues of Plato* (Random House, Inc., 1937), Vol. I, pp. 385–386. Used by permission of Random House, Inc., and Oxford University Press, Inc.

11. Isaiah 40:12-14, 21-22.

12. Bertrand Russell, *Mysticism and Logic* (Longmans, Green & Co., Inc., 1919), p. 106. Used by permission of Longmans, Green & Co., Inc., and George Allen and Unwin, Ltd., London.

13. Bertrand Russell, *A History of Western Philosophy* (Simon and Schuster, Inc., 1948), p. 567. Copyright, 1948, by Bertrand Russell. Used by permission of Simon and Schuster, Inc.

14. Walter E. Stuermann, "Are There Empirical Roots for the Law of Non-Contradiction?" *ETC.: A Review of General Semantics*, XIII, 4; "The Triune Nature of the Laws of Thought," *ETC.*, XV, 1.

Selected Bibliography

Bergson, Henri, *Creative Evolution*. Modern Library, Inc., 1944.
Boman, Thorlief, *Hebrew Thought Compared with Greek,* tr. by Jules L. Moreau. The Westminster Press, 1960.
Burtt, E. A., *Metaphysical Foundations of Modern Physical Science*. Doubleday and Co., Inc., 1955. Paperback.
—— *Types of Religious Philosophy*. Revised edition. Harper & Brothers, 1951.
Churchman, C. West, *Elements of Logic and Formal Science*. J. B. Lippincott Company, 1940.
Copi, I. M., *Introduction to Logic*. Second edition. The Macmillan Company, 1961.
Du Noüy, Lecomte, *Human Destiny*. Longmans, Green & Co., Inc., 1947.
Eves, Howard, and Newsom, C. V., *An Introduction to the Foundations and Fundamental Concepts of Mathematics*. Rinehart & Company, 1958.
Feigl, Herbert, and Brodbeck, May, *Readings in the Philosophy of Science*. Appleton-Century-Crofts, Inc., 1953.
Flew, Antony, and MacIntyre, Alasdair, *New Essays in Philosophical Theology*. The Macmillan Company, 1956.
Frank, Philipp, *Philosophy of Science*. Prentice-Hall, Inc., 1957.
Heim, Karl, *Christian Faith and Natural Science*. Harper & Brothers, 1957. Paperback.
James, William, *Pragmatism*. Longmans, Green & Co., Inc., 1925.
—— *Varieties of Religious Experience*. Modern Library, Inc., n. d.
Kaufmann, W. A., *Nietzsche: Philosopher, Psychologist, Antichrist*. Princeton University Press, 1950.
Kline, Morris, *Mathematics and the Physical World*. The Thomas Y. Crowell Co., 1959.
Langer, Susanne K., *An Introduction to Symbolic Logic*. Dover

Publications, Inc., 1953. Paperback.

———— *Philosophy in a New Key.* Mentor Books, 1955. Paperback.

Moreau, Jules L., *Language and Religious Language* (Westminster Studies in Christian Communication, general editor, Kendig Brubaker Cully). The Westminster Press, 1961.

Pepper, Stephen C., *World Hypotheses.* University of California Press, 1942.

Popper, Karl R., *The Logic of Scientific Discovery.* Basic Books, Inc., 1959.

Raven, Charles E., *Natural Religion and Christian Theology.* Cambridge University Press, 1953.

Reichenbach, Hans, *The Rise of Scientific Philosophy.* University of California Press, 1956. Paperback.

Russell, Bertrand, *Introduction to Mathematical Philosophy.* The Macmillan Company, 1919.

———— *Mysticism and Logic and Other Essays.* George Allen and Unwin, Ltd., London, 1951.

———— *Religion and Science.* Oxford University Press, 1953.

Schleiermacher, Friedrich, *On Religion.* Harper & Brothers, 1958. Paperback.

Schweitzer, Albert, *Pilgrimage to Humanity,* tr. by W. E. Stuermann. Philosophical Library, Inc., 1961.

Sinclair, W. A., *An Introduction to Philosophy.* Oxford University Press, 1944.

Spinoza, Benedict, *Theologico-Political Treatise* in *The Chief Works of Benedict de Spinoza,* I. Dover Publications, Inc., 1951. Paperback.

Stuermann, W. E., and Hill, Johnson D., *Philosophy and the American Heritage.* Philosophical Library, Inc., 1961.

———— *Organized Labor: A Philosophical Perspective.* The Exposition Press, 1962.

Tsanoff, R. A., *The Nature of Evil.* The Macmillan Company, 1931.

Warbeke, J. H., *The Searching Mind of Greece.* F. S. Crofts, 1930.

Werkmeister, W. H., *The Basis and Structure of Knowledge.* Harper & Brothers, 1948.

Index